Five Times Five Is Not Ten

Make Multiplication Easy

Susan Greenwald, M.A. Ed.

LP **LONGEVITY PUBLISHING, LLC**
Englewood, Colorado • www.longevitypublishing.com

This book has been a labor of love
for students of all ages,
and will continue to be beneficial
for as long as children need to memorize math facts.

For Madison Olivia, with love.

Five Times Five Is Not Ten:
Make Multiplication Easy
LP 400

Copyright © 2008 by Susan Greenwald
All rights reserved.
Printed in U.S.A. by Sheridan Books on acid-free paper

Longevity Publishing LLC
Englewood, Colorado
www.longevitypublishing.com
ISBN 13: 978-0-9777323-1-9
10 9 8 7 6 5 4

First printing 2008
Second printing 2009
Third printing 2011

Edited by: Ellen Raymond
Design by: DBS, Inc.
Cover Design by: Lee Lewis Walsh, Words Plus Design

With the permission of Teacher Created Resources, some strategy names and concepts are used in this book that have appeared previously in **How to Teach Math Facts** *by Susan Greenwald.*

Table of Contents

Introduction iv

How to Use This Book v

Types of Workbook Pages viii

Guide to Introducing the Facts ix

Workbook Pages

• 1 Group 1

• Doubles 5

• Zero 13

• Count by 3s 17

• Count 5, 6, 7, 8 21

• I See 2 5s 25

• 4 Fingers 29

• More Count by 3s 37

• Pretend to Add with 9 41

• Rhymes 53

• Fives 61

• More Pretend to Add with 9 67

• See 2 4s 75

• More 4 Fingers 81

• Pretend to Add 93

• More Fives 101

• REVIEW 105

• More Fives 111

• More 4 Fingers 115

• STRETCH 119

• Think of 7×7 125

• More Pretend to Add with 9 129

• REVIEW 133

Answers 149

Certificate of Mastery 152

Math Facts Baseline Recorder 153

Record-Keeping Checklist 154

Index of Facts by Name 155

Multiplication Facts Listed by Name 156

Introduction

Five Times Five Is Not Ten: Make Multiplication Easy is a practical supplementary workbook to teach the multiplication facts to students. It includes strategies from my first book, *How to Teach Math Facts,* published in 1999 by Teacher Created Resources.

Designed for any age student who needs to memorize, learn, remember, master, or become fluent with the multiplication facts, *Five Times Five Is Not Ten* introduces the facts with easy-to-learn strategies, because mastery of basic math facts is essential for success in computation skills and solving word problems. For this reason, the workbook pages were intentionally not designated for a particular grade level.

> **The 148 reproducible practice pages will appeal to:**
> - Beginners
> - Elementary school children needing instruction, practice, or review of the math facts
> - Children in remedial programs
> - Children in accelerated programs who need to memorize math facts
> - Children with math disabilities
> - Older students who still struggle because they just never memorized the math facts

★ Classroom teachers, ★ parents, ★ home schooling educators, ★ resource room teachers, and ★ tutors will appreciate that:

- Lessons can be easily individualized for different learning abilities.
- Most of the pages are divided into two sections so that half sheets can be assigned.
- Samplings of addition and/or subtraction facts are mixed into some multiplication workbook pages to provide some review of addition and subtraction facts while learning multiplication.
- Children will remember multiplication facts because they are learning and reviewing with strategies, written practice, and math fact cards.
- Math assignments will be completed with confidence, and students will enjoy their success.

If you used *Two Plus Two Is Not Five: Easy Methods to Learn Addition and Subtraction,* the workbook written to help children remember addition and subtraction facts, you will notice these changes in *Five Times Five Is Not Ten.*

- Math facts are still introduced by names, but are referred to as *strategies,* rather than "tricks." Facts will be practiced, as in the previous book, by their names.
- The **Guide to Introducing the Facts** is new to this book. Parents and teachers can use the brief scripted instructions to assign new facts and workbook pages.
- **How to Use This Book** offers new suggestions for classroom teachers.

Enjoy teaching math!
Susan Greenwald, M.A. Ed.

How to Use This Book

Before we can ask children to memorize any of the multiplication facts, they need to

- Count to at least 81.
- Show what numbers mean. (The number 48 means 48 items.)
- Demonstrate understanding of multiplication. (6×8: Show 6×8 as *6 groups of 8,* and be able to count out the 48 items.)
- Be able to tell a word math or story problem related to the fact being taught. (6×8: There are six plates. Each plate has eight cookies on it. How many cookies are there in all?)

Excluding the Zero facts, there are twelve names or strategies to help remember the 81 multiplication facts. Some names might sound confusing or hard to learn, but children will remember the facts by the different names. If children recall the name, I See 2 5s as "2 5s" or "See 2 5s," that is perfectly okay. Likewise, Count 5,6,7,8 may be remembered as "Count" or just "5,6,7,8" and Pretend to Add with 9 may be referred to as "The 9s" or "9 Family." As long as children remember the facts, it does not matter if the exact name is recalled.

As you are introducing new multiplication strategies, you may want to refer to the **Guide to Introducing the Facts** and the following instructions.

For use with beginners who need to learn all of the multiplication facts:
Start with workbook page 1, and begin with step 3 on the following page.

For use with individuals or when working with small groups:
Begin with step 1 on the following page.

For use by a classroom teacher with a whole class of students who already know some math facts:

A. Use **Cumulative Practice** pages to help determine which facts your students know, and which ones they need to learn. Choose from pages 31, 44, 52, 65, 66, 79, 100, 124, 147, or 148 and give a timed math pretest. Pages nearer to the beginning of the book will test fewer facts than those at the end. There are 56 problems on each of these pages. (If you typically give children 3 minutes to complete 100 problems, then 1 minute and 40 seconds would be about right for 56 problems.)

B. Encourage your students to answer *only the ones they know without counting,* and to skip over and leave the others blank. Tell them you are doing this to find out which ones they know, so that you can teach them the ones they do not know. **Known** facts are those multiplication facts that are answered quickly and correctly. Children should not count to get an answer.

C. Use a clean copy of that test page to keep a tally of students who are stuck on particular facts. For example, on Page 31, if 16 students did not know the answer to 3×4, then mark 16 on top of that fact. If only one student did not know or had recorded a wrong answer for 2×2, mark 1 on top of that fact.

D. Transfer this data to page 154 under *Notes* on the **Record-Keeping Checklist**. Look at this information to see where to begin in the workbook. The workbook is designed to be used in sequence, so start with the first workbook page number on which students need to learn facts.

E. Start with step 3 below to introduce new facts. Set the pace according to your class and, if possible, divide the class into smaller groups to provide some individualization.

Steps to Teach the Math Facts

1. Use a set of multiplication flash cards to test the child to determine the **Baseline** of which facts are known.

2. **Known** facts are those multiplication facts that are answered quickly and correctly. Children should not count to get an answer.

   Record those known facts on the **Math Facts Baseline Recorder** provided on page 153. Then transfer the information to the **Record-Keeping Checklist** on page 154. After marking the known facts, unmarked spaces allow you to see easily which facts need to be learned. The workbook is designed to be used in sequence, so start with the first workbook page number where there are unmarked spaces.

3. Use counting items such as cubes, buttons, or paper clips for the initial introduction of the math fact with its strategy.

   Children need to demonstrate understanding of the meaning of multiplication before we ask them to memorize the facts.

4. As new facts are introduced, be sure to mark the **Record-Keeping Checklist**. Seeing those filled-in spaces will give children a feeling of accomplishment!

5. Practice should be scheduled at least three times per week; daily is best.

   The workbook includes 33 sets of introductions and was designed to introduce a new set of facts on each lesson day, but this does not necessarily mean every day.

The pace should be set by the student's ability. Not all children will be ready to advance at the same rate. Some will be able to handle one set of new facts in a day; others may need more time. Children in accelerated programs could be introduced to new facts at a faster pace.

As math facts are mastered, teachers can integrate them into the rest of the math curriculum.

Math Fact Cards

6. The math fact cards to be assigned are listed on the **Record-Keeping Checklist** and in the **Guide to Introducing the Facts**.

As each set of math facts is introduced, use 3″ by 5″ blank index cards to make math fact cards. Cards for known facts can be also be made for practice.

Parents are encouraged to provide daily practice at home with a set of math fact cards.

Teachers working 1:1 with children can incorporate practice of the math fact cards into their daily program.

Assign Pages

7. Following the introductory practice page for the new facts, allow the children to complete the practice pages. These pages provide application and review between the introductions of new facts.

Teachers can assign these practice pages for class work and/or homework.

Children should complete at least part if not all of each of the **Cumulative Practice** and **Review** pages. This ensures that they will not forget previously taught facts.

Use Strategy Names

8. Encourage use of the strategy name.

It is important for children to associate a fact with a strategy rather than count out an answer on fingers.

When stuck on a math fact, they should be reminded to think of the strategy and state the strategy name to recall the answer.

Review

9. Facts are reviewed throughout the book by themselves or in a variety of combinations.

10. Celebrate when all the math facts are mastered!

Types of Workbook Pages

There are four basic types of practice. Not all children will need to complete each page in its entirety. Most of the practice pages are divided into a top and bottom section so that shorter half-page tasks can easily be given.

Samplings of addition and/or subtraction facts are mixed into some multiplication workbook pages to:

- Provide students with some review of addition and subtraction facts while learning multiplication.
- Require children to focus on whether the problem is a multiplication, addition, or subtraction fact.

Introduction

These pages use a name or strategy to teach the new multiplication facts and may include a few previously taught facts. After an initial explanation, all children needing to learn the facts should complete this type of practice page. These pages may include some addition and/or subtraction facts.

Practice

These pages include the newly taught multiplication facts and/or a mixture of these newest math facts along with those from one or more other strategies previously taught. Most children will need to do all of these pages, while others need only complete parts of them. These pages may include some addition and/or subtraction facts.

Cumulative Practice

This type of practice page may follow the introduction and practice pages of newly taught facts. The children will be checked on the newly learned facts and most of the facts and strategies that have been taught previously. All children should complete these workbook pages, which are offered periodically throughout the book. These pages may include some addition and/or subtraction facts.

Review

These practice pages offer review of particular strategies and math facts. Not all students will need to do all of these pages. Some children will need to complete all of them, while others need only complete some of them to demonstrate mastery.

Guide to Introducing the Facts

- In a multiplication fact, the numbers being multiplied are called **factors**. The **product** is the answer or result of multiplying those numbers. Multiplication is **commutative**, meaning the order of the factors does not matter. $3 \times 4 = 4 \times 3$. These factors are 3 and 4. This product or answer is 12.

- Wherever **n** is written in place of a number, it represents any **n**umber.

- Rather than spelling out the number words in the phrases such as "two groups of six," I have intentionally written the numerals such as *2 groups of 6.*

- Throughout the book, compare the differences between fact pairs. For example, 3×6 has the same answer as 6×3, but the facts are represented differently.

18 stars in 3 groups of 6    **18 stars in 6 groups of 3**

- Whenever it says, "Direct students to show . . . ," students should use any kind of manipulative such as counters, crayons, cubes, or buttons to represent the multiplication fact. Or, students may draw lines, dots, or other shapes to show representations of the different math facts.

Manipulatives for 2 × 6    **Lines drawn for 2 × 6**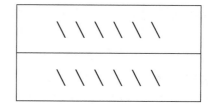

- Practice pages may include addition and/or subtraction facts mixed with the multiplication facts. Direct attention to the signs, and explain and show with manipulatives that these signs mean different things.

$$4 \times 1, \ 4 + 1, \ 4 - 1 \quad \text{or} \quad 7 \times 3, \ 7 + 3, \ 7 - 3$$

- If using flash cards to offer students another form of practice, the cards to add are listed in parenthesis after the page number.

Page 1: (1×1, 1×2, 1×3, 1×4, 1×5, 1×6, 1×7, 1×8, 1×9) Tell students to read the math fact as 1 group of **n**. Direct students to use manipulatives to show *1 group of 1, 1 group of 2, 1 group of 4, 1 group of 9,* and so on.

Page 2: (2×1, 3×1, 4×1, 5×1, 6×1, 7×1, 8×1, 9×1) Direct children to use manipulatives to show that these fact pairs equal the same answer. *1 group of 2 is the same 2 as in 2 groups of 1, 1 group of 3 is the same 3 as in 3 groups of 1, 1 group of 4 is the same 4 as in 4 groups of 1,* and so on.

- **Students need to know the answers to the Doubles addition facts before asking them to learn the <u>Doubles</u> multiplication facts.**

Page 5: (2×2, 2×3, 2×4, 2×5) Direct students to use manipulatives to show *2 groups of 2.* Hold out your two hands, palms up, and direct a student to place *1 group of 2* in each hand. Put your two hands together, and have the student count how many there are. Note that this is the same as doubling or adding $2 + 2$. Do the same for *2 groups of 3 =* the Double $3 + 3$, *2 groups of 4 =* the Double $4 + 4$, and *2 groups of 5 =* the Double $5 + 5$. This is counting by 2s.

Page 7: (3×2, 4×2, 5×2) Direct children to use manipulatives to show that each of these fact pairs equals the same answer. *2 groups of 3* is the same 6 as in *3 groups of 2, 2 groups of 4* is the same 8 as in *4 groups of 2*, and *2 groups of 5* is the same 10 as in *5 groups of 2*.

- **Pages 9 and 10 are designed to be introduced in the same lesson.**

Page 9: (2×6, 2×7, 2×8, 2×9) Follow page 5 directions to show *2 groups of 6* = the Double 6+6, *2 groups of 7* = the Double 7+7, *2 groups of 8* = the Double 8+8, and *2 groups of 9* = the Double 9+9.

Page 10: (6×2, 7×2, 8×2, 9×2) Follow page 7 directions for 2×6 and 6×2, 2×7 and 7×2, 2×8 and 8×2, and 2×9 and 9×2.

Pages 13 and 15: (1×0, 2×0, 3×0, 4×0, 5×0, 6×0, 7×0, 8×0, 9×0) (0×1, 0×2, 0×3, 0×4, 0×5, 0×6, 0×7, 0×8, 0×9) You may opt to assign only a few <u>Zero</u> fact cards rather than all of them.
　Introduce <u>Zero</u> with the concept of money, toys, or food—something that has meaning to them. Tell the student:
"I have five wallets filled with <u>Zero</u> dollars!" or
"I have six bags filled with <u>Zero</u> toys!" or
"I have <u>Zero</u> bowls filled with 1,000 chocolate candies!"
After each statement, ask the student how much they have, and they ought to realize that they have zero or nothing.

Page 17: (3×3) Direct children to use manipulatives to show *3 groups of 3*. Place two of the 3s together to show 3+3=6. Add on the other 3 to get 9. ⬚3⬚3⬚ + ⬚3⬚ This is the same as 6+3 and 3+6.

Page 21: (7×8, 8×7) Direct students to show *7 groups of 8*, and have them count out the 56 items. Then have students use the same counters to show *8 groups of 7*. Say you will show them a shortcut to remember 7×8 and 8×7 so it will not take so long next time to get the answer. Ask what two numbers are in sequence before 7 and 8. ___, ___, 7, 8. The responses **5** and **6** give the digits for the answer **56**. Remember this by "<u>Count 5,6,7,8.</u>"

Page 25: (5×5) Direct students to show **5** groups of **5**, and count by 5s for the answer. The two fives, or **2 5s**, in the fact 5×5 help them to remember this fact and its answer, 25, by saying, "<u>I See 2 5s</u> in 5×5."

- **The six sets of <u>4 Fingers</u> show an easy way to remember the facts by use of <u>Doubles</u>.**

Page 29: (3×4, 4×3) Direct children to use manipulatives to show *4 groups of 3*. Place *1 group of 3* at the end of each of four fingers. Manipulate the four fingers into a V, so that (left) two fingers have *2 groups of 3*, and the (right) two fingers have *2 groups of 3*. Ask: How many counters are on the two (left) fingers? How many on the other two fingers? What is 6+6? Then, use the same manipulatives to show that *4 groups of 3* is the same as *3 groups of 4*.

Page 29

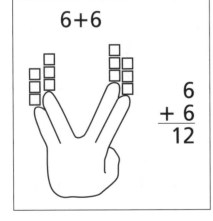

6+6

$$\begin{array}{r} 6 \\ + 6 \\ \hline 12 \end{array}$$

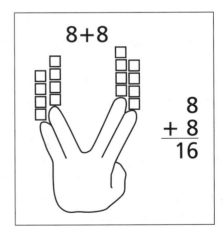

8+8

Page 33

$$\begin{array}{r} 8 \\ + 8 \\ \hline 16 \end{array}$$

Page 33: (4×4) Follow page 29 directions to show *4 groups of 4*. Place *1 group of 4* at the end of each of four fingers. Manipulate the four fingers into a V, so that two fingers have *2 groups of 4*, and the other two fingers have *2 groups of 4*. 8+8=16.

Page 37: (3×6, 6×3) Ask, "What is 3×3?" Direct students to show *6 groups of 3*. Divide the six groups in half to get two clusters. $\boxed{3\,|\,3\,|\,3}$=9 $\boxed{3\,|\,3\,|\,3}$=9 Show how 9+9=18. Remember these facts by saying, "3, 6, 9; 9+9 is 18."

- **The seven sets of <u>Pretend to Add with 9</u> facts are based on addition and subtraction fact families of 9, and the addition facts with 9+n and n+9.** (Magic 9 is an addition strategy in the book, *Two Plus Two is Not Five.*)

Page 41: (9×9) Students must know: 9+9, and 8+<u>1</u>=9 or 9−8=<u>1</u>. Direct students to show *9 groups of 9*, and have them count out the 81 items. Say you will show them a way to remember 9×9 so it will not take so long next time to get the answer. Pretend to add 9+9. You hear the "**eight**" sound from **eight**een. **8+ ?** equals 9. **8+1**, which gives us the two digits, **81**, for the answer.

Page 45: (9×7, 7×9) Follow page 41 directions. Students must know: 9+7 and 7+9, and 6+<u>3</u>=9 or 9−6=<u>3</u>. Direct students to show *9 groups of 7*, and have them count out the 63 items. Pretend to add 9+7. You hear the "**six**" sound from **six**teen. **6+ ?** equals 9. **6+3**, which gives us the two digits, **63**, for the answer.

Page 49: (9×4, 4×9) Follow page 41 directions. Students must know: 9+4 and 4+9, and 3+<u>6</u>=9 or 9−3=<u>6</u>. Direct students to show *9 groups of 4*, and have them count out the 36 items. Pretend to add 9+4. You hear the "**thir**" sound from **thir**teen. **3+ ?** equals 9. **3+6**, which gives us the two digits, **36**, for the answer. To show another strategy, ask the students, "What is 3×4?" They know 12 is the answer. Place the *groups of 4* so they are in clusters of three. Students can then add 12+12+12 to get 36. $\boxed{4\,|\,4\,|\,4}$=12 $\boxed{4\,|\,4\,|\,4}$=12 $\boxed{4\,|\,4\,|\,4}$=12

- **Some strategies require knowing how to cut a number in half.**

Page 53: (6×6) Direct students to show *6 groups of 6*, and have them count out the 36 items. Tap out the rhyme to remember this fact. "Six times six is 36." Students must know that six cut in half is three. The 3 is the first digit in the answer, and the 6 ends the rhyme.

Page 57: (6×8, 8×6) Direct students to show *6 groups of 8*, and have them count out the 48 items. Tap out the rhyme to remember this fact. "Six times eight is 48." Students must know that eight cut in half is four. The 4 is the first digit in the answer, and the 8 ends the rhyme.

Page 61: (3×5, 5×3) This fact pair must be memorized. Show the pattern of counting by 5s. 1 five = **5**, 2 fives = 1**0**, 3 fives = 1**5**, 4 fives = 2**0**, 5 fives = 2**5**. Products of 5 multiplied by an odd number (1, 3, 5, 7, 9) result with a numeral **5** in the ones place.

Page 67: (9×6, 6×9) Follow page 41 directions. Students must know: 9+6 and 6+9, and 5+<u>4</u>=9 or 9−5=<u>4</u>. Direct students to show *9 groups of 6*, and have them count out the 54 items. Pretend to add 9+6. You hear the "**fif**" sound from **fif**teen. **5+ ?** equals 9. **5+4**, which gives us the two digits, **54**, for the answer. To show another strategy, ask the students, "What is 3 × 6?" They know 18 is the answer. Place the *groups of 6* so they are in clusters of three. Students can then add 18+18+18 to get 54. $\boxed{6\,|\,6\,|\,6}$=18 $\boxed{6\,|\,6\,|\,6}$=18 $\boxed{6\,|\,6\,|\,6}$=18

Page 71: (9×5, 5×9) Follow page 41 directions. Students must know: 9+5 and 5+9, and 4+<u>5</u>=9 or 9−4=<u>5</u>. Direct students to show *9 groups of 5*, and have them count out the 45 items. Pretend to add 9+5. You hear the "**four**" sound from **four**teen. **4+ ?** equals 9. **4+5**, which gives us the two digits, **45**, for the answer. To show another strategy, ask the students, "What is 3×5?" They know 15 is the answer. Place the *groups of 5* so they are in clusters of three. Students can then add 15+15+15 to get 45. $\boxed{5\,|\,5\,|\,5}$=15 $\boxed{5\,|\,5\,|\,5}$=15 $\boxed{5\,|\,5\,|\,5}$=15

Page 75: (8×3, 3×8) Direct students to show **8** groups of **3**. Ask, "What is 4×3?" Divide the eight groups in half to get **2** clusters of **4**. $\boxed{3\,|\,3\,|\,3\,|\,3}$=12 $\boxed{3\,|\,3\,|\,3\,|\,3}$=12 Show how 12+12=24. Another strategy to remember this fact and its answer, **24**, is "<u>See 2 4s</u>." Cut the eight in half to get **two fours**. (4+4=8)

- **The remaining sets of <u>4 Fingers</u> require mentally doubling 10+10=20, 12+12=24, 14+14=28, and 16+16=32.**

Page 81: (4×5, 5×4) Follow page 29 directions to show *4 groups of 5*. Place *1 group of 5* at the end of each of four fingers. Manipulate the four fingers into a V, so that two fingers have *2 groups of 5*, and the other two fingers have *2 groups of 5*. 10+10=20.

Page 85: (4×6, 6×4) Follow page 29 directions to show *4 groups of 6*. Place *1 group of 6* at the end of each of four fingers. Manipulate the four fingers into a V, so that two fingers have *2 groups of 6*, and the other two fingers have *2 groups of 6*. 12+12=24.

Page 89: (4×7, 7×4) Follow page 29 directions to show *4 groups of 7*. Place *1 group of 7* at the end of each of four fingers. Manipulate the four fingers into a V, so that two fingers have *2 groups of 7*, and the other two fingers have *2 groups of 7*. 14+14=28.

Page 93: (7×7) Students must know: 7+7. Direct students to show *7 groups of 7*, and have them count out the 49 items. Say you will show them a way to remember 7×7 so it will not take so long next time to get the answer. Pretend to add 7+7. You hear the "**four**" sound from **four**teen. Sevens *look* a bit like *9* which gives us the other digit in the two digits, **49,** for the answer.

Page 97: (8×8) Students must know: 8+8. Direct students to show *8 groups of 8*, and have them count out the 64 items. Say you will show them a way to remember 8×8 so it will not take so long next time to get the answer. Pretend to add 8+8. You hear the "**six**" sound from **six**teen. If we cut eight in half, we get **4**, which gives us the other digit in the two digits, **64,** for the answer.

Page 101: (6×5, 5×6, 8×5, 5×8) Show the pattern of counting by 5s. 1 five = 5, 2 fives = 10, 3 fives = 15, 4 fives = 20, 5 fives = 25, 6 fives = 30, 7 fives = 35, 8 fives = 40, 9 fives = 45. Products of 5 multiplied by an even number (0, 2, 4, 6, 8) result with a numeral **0** in the ones place. If we cut six in half, we get **3**, which gives us the other digit in the two digits, **30,** for the answer to 6×5. If we cut eight in half, we get **4**, which gives us the other digit in the two digits, **40**, for the answer to 8×5.

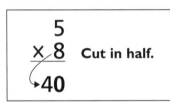

Page 111: (7×5, 5×7) Direct students to show *6 groups of 5*. Ask, "What is 6×5?" Direct students to add on another *group of 5* so there are *7 groups of 5*, and then count how much they have. 30 + 5 = 35. Also, use directions from page 61, and show the pattern of counting by 5s. 1 five = **5**, 2 fives = 10, 3 fives = 15, 4 fives = 20, 5 fives = **25**, 6 fives = 30, 7 fives = **35**.

Page 115: (4×8, 8×4) Follow page 29 directions to show *4 groups of 8*. Place *1 group of 8* at the end of each of four fingers. Manipulate the four fingers into a V, so that two fingers have *2 groups of 8*, and the other two fingers have *2 groups of 8*. 16+16=32.

Page 119: (3×7, 7×3) Direct students to show *3 groups of 7*, and have them count out the 21 items. Then ask students to use the same counters to show *7 groups of 3*. Say there is an easy way to remember these facts if they "stretch" their imagination. Use a piece of yarn, cooked spaghetti, or a cut rubber band to show how the factors 3 and 7 stretch into the answer. Change 3 into a **2**, and 7 into a **1** to get the two digits, **21**, for the answer.

Page 125: (6×7, 7×6) Ask, "What is 7×7?" Direct students to show *7 groups of 7*, and to tell what they would have left if they took away *1 group of 7*. There would be only *6 groups of 7*, or 42. Students will "Think of 7×7" to remember this set of facts. 6×7 is one less seven than 7×7. 49−7=**42**. To show another strategy, ask the students, "What is 3×7?" They know 21 is the answer. Divide the six groups in half to get two clusters. Show how 21+21=42. ⬚7⎸7⎸7⬚=21 ⬚7⎸7⎸7⬚=21

Page 129: (9×8, 8×9, 9×3, 3×9) Follow page 41 directions. Students must know: 9+8 and 8+9, and 7+<u>2</u>=9 or 9−7=<u>2</u>. Direct students to show *9 groups of 8*, and have them count out the 72 items. Pretend to add 9+8. You hear the "**seven**" sound from **seven**teen. **7+ ?** equals 9. **7+2**, which gives us the two digits, **72**, for the answer. Students must know: 9+3 and 3+9, and 2+<u>7</u>=9 or 9−2=<u>7</u>. Direct students to show *9 groups of 3*, and have them count out the 27 items. Pretend to add 9+3. You hear the "**twe**" sound from **twe**lve. **2+ ?** equals 9. **2+7**, which gives us the two digits, **27**, for the answer.

1 Group

The answer for any number multiplied by 1 is that number.

1 group of 3 is 3.   1 group of 8 is 8.   Draw 1 group of 6.

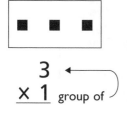   2 ⨉4 = 8

3
× 1 group of

8
× 1 group of

6
× 1 group of

Practice **1 Group**.

2
× 1 group of

5
× 1 group of

4
× 1 group of

1
× 1 group of

9
× 1 group of

Practice **1 Group** with addition. Watch + and × signs.

5
× 1

1
+ 1

9
× 1

3
× 1

8
+ 1

7
× 1

6
+ 1

6
× 1

2
× 1

4
+ 1

8
× 1

9
+ 1

3
+ 1

4
× 1

Practice **1 Group** with subtraction. Watch − and × signs.

3
× 1

9
− 1

5
× 1

8
× 1

7
− 1

4
− 1

1
× 1

6
− 1

7
× 1

8
− 1

3
− 1

6
× 1

5
− 1

4
× 1

More 1 Group

These answers are the same.

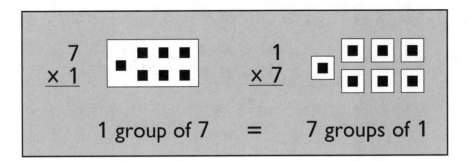

1 group of 7   =   7 groups of 1

Draw 1 group of 4.

$\begin{array}{r} 4 \\ \times\ 1 \end{array}$ group of

Draw 4 groups of 1.

$\begin{array}{r} 1 \\ \times\ 4 \end{array}$ groups of

Practice **1 Group**.

6 × 1	1 × 6	9 × 1	1 × 9	7 × 1	1 × 7	1 × 1
2 × 1	1 × 5	1 × 4	3 × 1	6 × 1	1 × 8	1 × 4
1 × 7	1 × 1	7 × 1	8 × 1	1 × 3	1 × 2	9 × 1
1 × 8	1 × 6	4 × 1	1 × 9	5 × 1	1 × 1	1 × 3

Name _____

Practice **1 Group** with addition.

8 × 1	1 + 8	1 + 4	1 × 7	1 × 3	2 × 1	5 + 1
1 × 9	1 × 1	1 + 1	6 × 1	1 × 5	6 + 1	1 × 4
3 × 1	9 + 1	1 × 2	1 + 3	9 × 1	7 × 1	1 × 8
7 + 1	1 × 6	4 × 1	5 × 1	2 + 1	1 × 1	1 + 6

Practice **1 Group** with subtraction this way.

$1 \times 7 =$ _____ $9 - 1 =$ _____ $1 \times 5 =$ _____ $4 \times 1 =$ _____

$6 - 1 =$ _____ $1 \times 3 =$ _____ $6 \times 1 =$ _____ $1 \times 9 =$ _____

$2 \times 1 =$ _____ $4 - 1 =$ _____ $8 \times 1 =$ _____ $1 \times 4 =$ _____

$8 - 1 =$ _____ $9 \times 1 =$ _____ $1 \times 1 =$ _____ $3 - 1 =$ _____

$1 \times 6 =$ _____ $5 - 1 =$ _____ $7 - 1 =$ _____ $7 \times 1 =$ _____

$5 \times 1 =$ _____ $1 \times 8 =$ _____ $2 - 1 =$ _____ $3 \times 1 =$ _____

Name _____

Practice **1 Group** with addition this way.

1×6= _____	6+1= _____	1×7= _____	8×1= _____
9×1= _____	1+1= _____	8+1= _____	4×1= _____
1+5= _____	2×1= _____	4+1= _____	1×9= _____
1×2= _____	1+3= _____	1×3= _____	5+1= _____
5×1= _____	9+1= _____	1+7= _____	1×1= _____
2+1= _____	1×8= _____	1×5= _____	7×1= _____

Practice **1 Group** with subtraction.

$$\begin{array}{r} 1 \\ \times\,3 \\ \hline \end{array} \qquad \begin{array}{r} 4 \\ \times\,1 \\ \hline \end{array} \qquad \begin{array}{r} 9 \\ -\,1 \\ \hline \end{array} \qquad \begin{array}{r} 5 \\ -\,1 \\ \hline \end{array} \qquad \begin{array}{r} 3 \\ \times\,1 \\ \hline \end{array} \qquad \begin{array}{r} 3 \\ -\,1 \\ \hline \end{array} \qquad \begin{array}{r} 1 \\ \times\,8 \\ \hline \end{array}$$

$$\begin{array}{r} 1 \\ \times\,6 \\ \hline \end{array} \qquad \begin{array}{r} 6 \\ -\,1 \\ \hline \end{array} \qquad \begin{array}{r} 5 \\ \times\,1 \\ \hline \end{array} \qquad \begin{array}{r} 1 \\ \times\,1 \\ \hline \end{array} \qquad \begin{array}{r} 4 \\ -\,1 \\ \hline \end{array} \qquad \begin{array}{r} 1 \\ \times\,9 \\ \hline \end{array} \qquad \begin{array}{r} 6 \\ \times\,1 \\ \hline \end{array}$$

$$\begin{array}{r} 2 \\ -\,1 \\ \hline \end{array} \qquad \begin{array}{r} 9 \\ \times\,1 \\ \hline \end{array} \qquad \begin{array}{r} 1 \\ \times\,3 \\ \hline \end{array} \qquad \begin{array}{r} 1 \\ \times\,5 \\ \hline \end{array} \qquad \begin{array}{r} 1 \\ \times\,4 \\ \hline \end{array} \qquad \begin{array}{r} 7 \\ \times\,1 \\ \hline \end{array} \qquad \begin{array}{r} 8 \\ -\,1 \\ \hline \end{array}$$

$$\begin{array}{r} 1 \\ \times\,2 \\ \hline \end{array} \qquad \begin{array}{r} 1 \\ \times\,7 \\ \hline \end{array} \qquad \begin{array}{r} 4 \\ \times\,1 \\ \hline \end{array} \qquad \begin{array}{r} 10 \\ -\,1 \\ \hline \end{array} \qquad \begin{array}{r} 8 \\ \times\,1 \\ \hline \end{array} \qquad \begin{array}{r} 2 \\ \times\,1 \\ \hline \end{array} \qquad \begin{array}{r} 7 \\ -\,1 \\ \hline \end{array}$$

Doubles

Think of 2 hands. 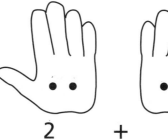 $\begin{array}{r} 2 \\ + 2 \\ \hline \end{array}$ or $\begin{array}{r} 2 \\ \times 2 \\ \hline \end{array}$ groups of

2 + 2

Think of 2 hands.  $\begin{array}{r} 3 \\ + 3 \\ \hline \end{array}$ or $\begin{array}{r} 3 \\ \times 2 \\ \hline \end{array}$ groups of $\begin{array}{r} 2 \\ 2 \\ + 2 \\ \hline 6 \end{array}$

6

3 + 3

Think of 2 hands. 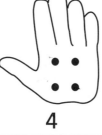 $\begin{array}{r} 4 \\ + 4 \\ \hline \end{array}$ or $\begin{array}{r} 4 \\ \times 2 \\ \hline \end{array}$ groups of

4 + 4

Think of 2 hands. 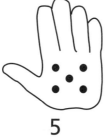 $\begin{array}{r} 5 \\ + 5 \\ \hline \end{array}$ or $\begin{array}{r} 5 \\ \times 2 \\ \hline \end{array}$ groups of

5 + 5

(You know 2 groups of 1. This is also **1 Group**: 2×1 and 1×2.)

Practice **Doubles**.

$\begin{array}{r} 4 \\ \times 2 \\ \hline \end{array}$ $\begin{array}{r} 5 \\ \times 2 \\ \hline \end{array}$ $\begin{array}{r} 3 \\ \times 2 \\ \hline \end{array}$ $\begin{array}{r} 5 \\ \times 2 \\ \hline \end{array}$ $\begin{array}{r} 2 \\ \times 2 \\ \hline \end{array}$ $\begin{array}{r} 4 \\ \times 2 \\ \hline \end{array}$ $\begin{array}{r} 1 \\ \times 2 \\ \hline \end{array}$

$\begin{array}{r} 2 \\ \times 2 \\ \hline \end{array}$ $\begin{array}{r} 3 \\ \times 2 \\ \hline \end{array}$ $\begin{array}{r} 1 \\ \times 2 \\ \hline \end{array}$ $\begin{array}{r} 4 \\ \times 2 \\ \hline \end{array}$ $\begin{array}{r} 1 \\ \times 2 \\ \hline \end{array}$ $\begin{array}{r} 5 \\ \times 2 \\ \hline \end{array}$ $\begin{array}{r} 3 \\ \times 2 \\ \hline \end{array}$

Name _____

Practice **Doubles** and **1 Group**.

5 × 2	2 × 2	1 × 1	5 × 1	3 × 2	4 × 2	3 × 1
1 × 6	1 × 4	5 × 2	4 × 2	2 × 2	1 × 2	3 × 2
4 × 2	3 × 2	2 × 1	2 × 2	5 × 2	4 × 1	5 × 2
1 × 3	1 × 5	2 × 2	7 × 1	4 × 2	3 × 2	9 × 1

Practice **Doubles** and **1 Group** with addition.

2×4= _____	6+1= _____	2×2= _____	1×6= _____
7×1= _____	1+1= _____	8+1= _____	2×3= _____
1+5= _____	2×1= _____	4+1= _____	9×1= _____
2×2= _____	1+3= _____	2×5= _____	1+7= _____
5×1= _____	2×3= _____	1×1= _____	9+1= _____
2+1= _____	1×8= _____	2×4= _____	2×5= _____

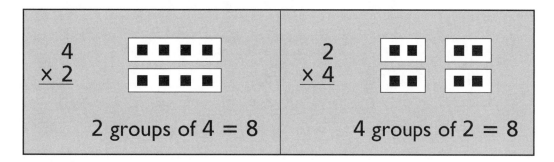

Name _____

More Doubles

These answers are the same.

$$\begin{array}{r} 4 \\ \times\ 2 \\ \hline \end{array}$$ ▪▪▪▪
▪▪▪▪

2 groups of 4 = 8

$$\begin{array}{r} 2 \\ \times\ 4 \\ \hline \end{array}$$ ▪▪ ▪▪
▪▪ ▪▪

4 groups of 2 = 8

Draw 2 groups of 3.

$$\begin{array}{r} 3 \\ \times\ 2 \end{array}$$ groups of

Draw 3 groups of 2.

$$\begin{array}{r} 2 \\ \times\ 3 \end{array}$$ groups of

Practice **Doubles**.

$$\begin{array}{r} 4 \\ \times\ 2 \\ \hline \end{array}$$
$$\begin{array}{r} 2 \\ \times\ 4 \\ \hline \end{array}$$
$$\begin{array}{r} 2 \\ \times\ 5 \\ \hline \end{array}$$
$$\begin{array}{r} 3 \\ \times\ 2 \\ \hline \end{array}$$
$$\begin{array}{r} 2 \\ \times\ 4 \\ \hline \end{array}$$
$$\begin{array}{r} 2 \\ \times\ 3 \\ \hline \end{array}$$
$$\begin{array}{r} 5 \\ \times\ 2 \\ \hline \end{array}$$

Practice **Doubles** and **1 Group**.

$$\begin{array}{r} 2 \\ \times\ 3 \\ \hline \end{array}$$
$$\begin{array}{r} 9 \\ \times\ 1 \\ \hline \end{array}$$
$$\begin{array}{r} 2 \\ \times\ 4 \\ \hline \end{array}$$
$$\begin{array}{r} 1 \\ \times\ 5 \\ \hline \end{array}$$
$$\begin{array}{r} 3 \\ \times\ 2 \\ \hline \end{array}$$
$$\begin{array}{r} 1 \\ \times\ 3 \\ \hline \end{array}$$
$$\begin{array}{r} 2 \\ \times\ 5 \\ \hline \end{array}$$

$$\begin{array}{r} 1 \\ \times\ 4 \\ \hline \end{array}$$
$$\begin{array}{r} 2 \\ \times\ 1 \\ \hline \end{array}$$
$$\begin{array}{r} 2 \\ \times\ 2 \\ \hline \end{array}$$
$$\begin{array}{r} 5 \\ \times\ 2 \\ \hline \end{array}$$
$$\begin{array}{r} 1 \\ \times\ 6 \\ \hline \end{array}$$
$$\begin{array}{r} 4 \\ \times\ 2 \\ \hline \end{array}$$
$$\begin{array}{r} 8 \\ \times\ 1 \\ \hline \end{array}$$

$$\begin{array}{r} 1 \\ \times\ 1 \\ \hline \end{array}$$
$$\begin{array}{r} 2 \\ \times\ 5 \\ \hline \end{array}$$
$$\begin{array}{r} 3 \\ \times\ 1 \\ \hline \end{array}$$
$$\begin{array}{r} 2 \\ \times\ 3 \\ \hline \end{array}$$
$$\begin{array}{r} 2 \\ \times\ 4 \\ \hline \end{array}$$
$$\begin{array}{r} 4 \\ \times\ 1 \\ \hline \end{array}$$
$$\begin{array}{r} 1 \\ \times\ 7 \\ \hline \end{array}$$

Name _____

Practice **Doubles** with addition.

$\begin{array}{r} 2 \\ \times\,5 \\ \hline \end{array}$	$\begin{array}{r} 4 \\ +\,4 \\ \hline \end{array}$	$\begin{array}{r} 2 \\ \times\,3 \\ \hline \end{array}$	$\begin{array}{r} 5 \\ \times\,2 \\ \hline \end{array}$	$\begin{array}{r} 2 \\ +\,2 \\ \hline \end{array}$	$\begin{array}{r} 2 \\ \times\,5 \\ \hline \end{array}$	$\begin{array}{r} 3 \\ +\,3 \\ \hline \end{array}$
$\begin{array}{r} 2 \\ \times\,2 \\ \hline \end{array}$	$\begin{array}{r} 4 \\ \times\,2 \\ \hline \end{array}$	$\begin{array}{r} 8 \\ +\,8 \\ \hline \end{array}$	$\begin{array}{r} 3 \\ \times\,2 \\ \hline \end{array}$	$\begin{array}{r} 5 \\ +\,5 \\ \hline \end{array}$	$\begin{array}{r} 2 \\ \times\,3 \\ \hline \end{array}$	$\begin{array}{r} 1 \\ +\,1 \\ \hline \end{array}$
$\begin{array}{r} 3 \\ \times\,2 \\ \hline \end{array}$	$\begin{array}{r} 5 \\ \times\,2 \\ \hline \end{array}$	$\begin{array}{r} 6 \\ +\,6 \\ \hline \end{array}$	$\begin{array}{r} 4 \\ +\,4 \\ \hline \end{array}$	$\begin{array}{r} 2 \\ \times\,4 \\ \hline \end{array}$	$\begin{array}{r} 2 \\ \times\,5 \\ \hline \end{array}$	$\begin{array}{r} 7 \\ +\,7 \\ \hline \end{array}$
$\begin{array}{r} 5 \\ +\,5 \\ \hline \end{array}$	$\begin{array}{r} 2 \\ \times\,2 \\ \hline \end{array}$	$\begin{array}{r} 2 \\ \times\,4 \\ \hline \end{array}$	$\begin{array}{r} 2 \\ \times\,5 \\ \hline \end{array}$	$\begin{array}{r} 3 \\ +\,3 \\ \hline \end{array}$	$\begin{array}{r} 4 \\ \times\,2 \\ \hline \end{array}$	$\begin{array}{r} 2 \\ \times\,3 \\ \hline \end{array}$

Practice **Doubles** with subtraction.

$\begin{array}{r} 3 \\ \times\,2 \\ \hline \end{array}$	$\begin{array}{r} 9 \\ -\,1 \\ \hline \end{array}$	$\begin{array}{r} 2 \\ \times\,4 \\ \hline \end{array}$	$\begin{array}{r} 5 \\ \times\,2 \\ \hline \end{array}$	$\begin{array}{r} 2 \\ \times\,3 \\ \hline \end{array}$	$\begin{array}{r} 4 \\ -\,1 \\ \hline \end{array}$	$\begin{array}{r} 2 \\ \times\,5 \\ \hline \end{array}$
$\begin{array}{r} 5 \\ -\,1 \\ \hline \end{array}$	$\begin{array}{r} 2 \\ \times\,2 \\ \hline \end{array}$	$\begin{array}{r} 2 \\ \times\,3 \\ \hline \end{array}$	$\begin{array}{r} 1 \\ \times\,2 \\ \hline \end{array}$	$\begin{array}{r} 5 \\ \times\,2 \\ \hline \end{array}$	$\begin{array}{r} 4 \\ \times\,2 \\ \hline \end{array}$	$\begin{array}{r} 8 \\ -\,1 \\ \hline \end{array}$
$\begin{array}{r} 2 \\ \times\,5 \\ \hline \end{array}$	$\begin{array}{r} 4 \\ \times\,2 \\ \hline \end{array}$	$\begin{array}{r} 2 \\ -\,1 \\ \hline \end{array}$	$\begin{array}{r} 3 \\ \times\,2 \\ \hline \end{array}$	$\begin{array}{r} 3 \\ -\,1 \\ \hline \end{array}$	$\begin{array}{r} 2 \\ \times\,5 \\ \hline \end{array}$	$\begin{array}{r} 2 \\ \times\,2 \\ \hline \end{array}$
$\begin{array}{r} 2 \\ \times\,4 \\ \hline \end{array}$	$\begin{array}{r} 7 \\ -\,1 \\ \hline \end{array}$	$\begin{array}{r} 1 \\ \times\,2 \\ \hline \end{array}$	$\begin{array}{r} 2 \\ \times\,5 \\ \hline \end{array}$	$\begin{array}{r} 6 \\ -\,1 \\ \hline \end{array}$	$\begin{array}{r} 2 \\ \times\,3 \\ \hline \end{array}$	$\begin{array}{r} 2 \\ \times\,4 \\ \hline \end{array}$

Name _____

More Doubles

Think of 2 hands.  $\begin{array}{r} 6 \\ + 6 \\ \hline \end{array}$ or $\begin{array}{r} 6 \\ \times 2 \\ \hline \end{array}$ groups of

 6   +   6

Think of 2 hands. 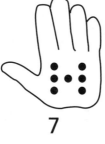 $\begin{array}{r} 7 \\ + 7 \\ \hline \end{array}$ or $\begin{array}{r} 7 \\ \times 2 \\ \hline \end{array}$ groups of

 7   +   7

Think of 2 hands.  $\begin{array}{r} 8 \\ + 8 \\ \hline \end{array}$ or $\begin{array}{r} 8 \\ \times 2 \\ \hline \end{array}$ groups of

 8   +   8

Think of 2 hands.  $\begin{array}{r} 9 \\ + 9 \\ \hline \end{array}$ or $\begin{array}{r} 9 \\ \times 2 \\ \hline \end{array}$ groups of

 9   +   9

Practice **Doubles**.

$\begin{array}{r} 7 \\ \times 2 \\ \hline \end{array}$ $\begin{array}{r} 9 \\ \times 2 \\ \hline \end{array}$ $\begin{array}{r} 8 \\ \times 2 \\ \hline \end{array}$ $\begin{array}{r} 6 \\ \times 2 \\ \hline \end{array}$ $\begin{array}{r} 9 \\ \times 2 \\ \hline \end{array}$ $\begin{array}{r} 7 \\ \times 2 \\ \hline \end{array}$ $\begin{array}{r} 8 \\ \times 2 \\ \hline \end{array}$

$\begin{array}{r} 8 \\ \times 2 \\ \hline \end{array}$ $\begin{array}{r} 7 \\ \times 2 \\ \hline \end{array}$ $\begin{array}{r} 9 \\ \times 2 \\ \hline \end{array}$ $\begin{array}{r} 8 \\ \times 2 \\ \hline \end{array}$ $\begin{array}{r} 6 \\ \times 2 \\ \hline \end{array}$ $\begin{array}{r} 9 \\ \times 2 \\ \hline \end{array}$ $\begin{array}{r} 6 \\ \times 2 \\ \hline \end{array}$

Name _____

More Doubles

These answers are the same.

$\begin{array}{r} 6 \\ \times 2 \\ \hline 12 \end{array}$ $\begin{array}{r} 2 \\ \times 6 \\ \hline 12 \end{array}$	$\begin{array}{r} 7 \\ \times 2 \\ \hline 14 \end{array}$ $\begin{array}{r} 2 \\ \times 7 \\ \hline 14 \end{array}$	$\begin{array}{r} 8 \\ \times 2 \\ \hline 16 \end{array}$ $\begin{array}{r} 2 \\ \times 8 \\ \hline 16 \end{array}$	$\begin{array}{r} 9 \\ \times 2 \\ \hline 18 \end{array}$ $\begin{array}{r} 2 \\ \times 9 \\ \hline 18 \end{array}$

Draw 2 groups of 6. | Draw 6 groups of 2.

$\begin{array}{r} 6 \\ \times 2 \end{array}$ groups of $\begin{array}{r} 2 \\ \times 6 \end{array}$ groups of

Practice Doubles.

$$\begin{array}{r} 2 \\ \times 8 \\ \hline \end{array} \quad \begin{array}{r} 3 \\ \times 2 \\ \hline \end{array} \quad \begin{array}{r} 2 \\ \times 7 \\ \hline \end{array} \quad \begin{array}{r} 2 \\ \times 9 \\ \hline \end{array} \quad \begin{array}{r} 2 \\ \times 2 \\ \hline \end{array} \quad \begin{array}{r} 6 \\ \times 2 \\ \hline \end{array} \quad \begin{array}{r} 2 \\ \times 5 \\ \hline \end{array}$$

$$\begin{array}{r} 7 \\ \times 2 \\ \hline \end{array} \quad \begin{array}{r} 2 \\ \times 9 \\ \hline \end{array} \quad \begin{array}{r} 2 \\ \times 4 \\ \hline \end{array} \quad \begin{array}{r} 8 \\ \times 2 \\ \hline \end{array} \quad \begin{array}{r} 4 \\ \times 2 \\ \hline \end{array} \quad \begin{array}{r} 2 \\ \times 7 \\ \hline \end{array} \quad \begin{array}{r} 2 \\ \times 3 \\ \hline \end{array}$$

$$\begin{array}{r} 2 \\ \times 6 \\ \hline \end{array} \quad \begin{array}{r} 9 \\ \times 2 \\ \hline \end{array} \quad \begin{array}{r} 2 \\ \times 5 \\ \hline \end{array} \quad \begin{array}{r} 2 \\ \times 7 \\ \hline \end{array} \quad \begin{array}{r} 2 \\ \times 8 \\ \hline \end{array} \quad \begin{array}{r} 5 \\ \times 2 \\ \hline \end{array} \quad \begin{array}{r} 2 \\ \times 6 \\ \hline \end{array}$$

$$\begin{array}{r} 2 \\ \times 3 \\ \hline \end{array} \quad \begin{array}{r} 8 \\ \times 2 \\ \hline \end{array} \quad \begin{array}{r} 2 \\ \times 9 \\ \hline \end{array} \quad \begin{array}{r} 4 \\ \times 2 \\ \hline \end{array} \quad \begin{array}{r} 6 \\ \times 2 \\ \hline \end{array} \quad \begin{array}{r} 2 \\ \times 8 \\ \hline \end{array} \quad \begin{array}{r} 7 \\ \times 2 \\ \hline \end{array}$$

Name _____

Practice **Doubles** and **1 Group**.

| $\begin{array}{r}2\\ \times 9\\ \hline\end{array}$ | $\begin{array}{r}4\\ \times 2\\ \hline\end{array}$ | $\begin{array}{r}9\\ \times 1\\ \hline\end{array}$ | $\begin{array}{r}8\\ \times 2\\ \hline\end{array}$ | $\begin{array}{r}2\\ \times 7\\ \hline\end{array}$ | $\begin{array}{r}1\\ \times 4\\ \hline\end{array}$ | $\begin{array}{r}9\\ \times 2\\ \hline\end{array}$ |

| $\begin{array}{r}1\\ \times 8\\ \hline\end{array}$ | $\begin{array}{r}6\\ \times 2\\ \hline\end{array}$ | $\begin{array}{r}2\\ \times 3\\ \hline\end{array}$ | $\begin{array}{r}2\\ \times 6\\ \hline\end{array}$ | $\begin{array}{r}1\\ \times 6\\ \hline\end{array}$ | $\begin{array}{r}2\\ \times 5\\ \hline\end{array}$ | $\begin{array}{r}2\\ \times 1\\ \hline\end{array}$ |

| $\begin{array}{r}2\\ \times 8\\ \hline\end{array}$ | $\begin{array}{r}1\\ \times 5\\ \hline\end{array}$ | $\begin{array}{r}7\\ \times 2\\ \hline\end{array}$ | $\begin{array}{r}6\\ \times 2\\ \hline\end{array}$ | $\begin{array}{r}2\\ \times 8\\ \hline\end{array}$ | $\begin{array}{r}2\\ \times 2\\ \hline\end{array}$ | $\begin{array}{r}7\\ \times 2\\ \hline\end{array}$ |

| $\begin{array}{r}3\\ \times 1\\ \hline\end{array}$ | $\begin{array}{r}2\\ \times 7\\ \hline\end{array}$ | $\begin{array}{r}2\\ \times 9\\ \hline\end{array}$ | $\begin{array}{r}7\\ \times 1\\ \hline\end{array}$ | $\begin{array}{r}9\\ \times 2\\ \hline\end{array}$ | $\begin{array}{r}8\\ \times 2\\ \hline\end{array}$ | $\begin{array}{r}2\\ \times 4\\ \hline\end{array}$ |

Practice this way.

$2 \times 8 =$ _____	$7 \times 2 =$ _____	$1 \times 8 =$ _____	$5 \times 2 =$ _____
$9 \times 1 =$ _____	$2 \times 3 =$ _____	$9 \times 2 =$ _____	$2 \times 1 =$ _____
$6 \times 2 =$ _____	$1 \times 4 =$ _____	$7 \times 1 =$ _____	$2 \times 7 =$ _____
$1 \times 1 =$ _____	$2 \times 4 =$ _____	$8 \times 2 =$ _____	$3 \times 1 =$ _____
$2 \times 2 =$ _____	$9 \times 2 =$ _____	$2 \times 6 =$ _____	$6 \times 2 =$ _____
$7 \times 2 =$ _____	$1 \times 6 =$ _____	$1 \times 5 =$ _____	$8 \times 2 =$ _____

Name _____

Practice **Doubles** with addition and subtraction.

2 $\times 3$	6 $+ 6$	8 $\times 2$	12 $- 6$	2 $\times 4$	7 $\times 2$	8 $- 4$
5 $\times 2$	2 $\times 7$	9 $+ 9$	2 $\times 8$	3 $+ 3$	2 $\times 9$	2 $\times 2$
7 $+ 7$	16 $- 8$	2 $\times 6$	5 $+ 5$	9 $\times 2$	10 $- 5$	8 $+ 8$
6 $\times 2$	2 $\times 9$	2 $\times 7$	6 $- 3$	18 $- 9$	2 $\times 8$	2 $\times 6$

Practice this way.

$2\times6=$ _____	$4+4=$ _____	$6\times2=$ _____	$12-6=$ _____
$9\times2=$ _____	$8+8=$ _____	$2\times7=$ _____	$2\times4=$ _____
$2+2=$ _____	$5\times2=$ _____	$10-5=$ _____	$2\times9=$ _____
$2\times3=$ _____	$4-2=$ _____	$6\times2=$ _____	$8\times2=$ _____
$14-7=$ _____	$7\times2=$ _____	$2\times8=$ _____	$3\times2=$ _____
$9+9=$ _____	$2\times5=$ _____	$9\times2=$ _____	$3+3=$ _____

Name _____

Zero

What if you have one box
filled with zero games?

How many games do
you have in the box?

You have none,
or zero.

$$\begin{array}{r} 0 \\ \times\ 1 \\ \hline \end{array}$$

What if you have five boxes
filled with zero million
dollars!!?

□ □ □ □ □

How much money do
you have in the boxes?

You have nothing,
or zero dollars.

$$\begin{array}{r} 0 \\ \times\ 5 \\ \hline \end{array}$$

The answer for any number multiplied by 0 is 0.

Practice **Zero**.

$\begin{array}{r} 0 \\ \times\ 2 \\ \hline \end{array}$	$\begin{array}{r} 0 \\ \times\ 3 \\ \hline \end{array}$	$\begin{array}{r} 0 \\ \times\ 9 \\ \hline \end{array}$	$\begin{array}{r} 0 \\ \times\ 8 \\ \hline \end{array}$	$\begin{array}{r} 0 \\ \times\ 4 \\ \hline \end{array}$	$\begin{array}{r} 0 \\ \times\ 7 \\ \hline \end{array}$	$\begin{array}{r} 0 \\ \times\ 6 \\ \hline \end{array}$

Practice **Zero** and **1 Group**.

$\begin{array}{r} 0 \\ \times\ 1 \\ \hline \end{array}$	$\begin{array}{r} 1 \\ \times\ 3 \\ \hline \end{array}$	$\begin{array}{r} 0 \\ \times\ 9 \\ \hline \end{array}$	$\begin{array}{r} 7 \\ \times\ 1 \\ \hline \end{array}$	$\begin{array}{r} 0 \\ \times\ 5 \\ \hline \end{array}$	$\begin{array}{r} 0 \\ \times\ 8 \\ \hline \end{array}$	$\begin{array}{r} 5 \\ \times\ 1 \\ \hline \end{array}$
$\begin{array}{r} 0 \\ \times\ 7 \\ \hline \end{array}$	$\begin{array}{r} 0 \\ \times\ 2 \\ \hline \end{array}$	$\begin{array}{r} 1 \\ \times\ 9 \\ \hline \end{array}$	$\begin{array}{r} 1 \\ \times\ 4 \\ \hline \end{array}$	$\begin{array}{r} 0 \\ \times\ 4 \\ \hline \end{array}$	$\begin{array}{r} 2 \\ \times\ 1 \\ \hline \end{array}$	$\begin{array}{r} 0 \\ \times\ 3 \\ \hline \end{array}$
$\begin{array}{r} 6 \\ \times\ 1 \\ \hline \end{array}$	$\begin{array}{r} 0 \\ \times\ 6 \\ \hline \end{array}$	$\begin{array}{r} 1 \\ \times\ 8 \\ \hline \end{array}$	$\begin{array}{r} 0 \\ \times\ 9 \\ \hline \end{array}$	$\begin{array}{r} 0 \\ \times\ 1 \\ \hline \end{array}$	$\begin{array}{r} 0 \\ \times\ 5 \\ \hline \end{array}$	$\begin{array}{r} 1 \\ \times\ 1 \\ \hline \end{array}$

Name _____

Practice **Zero** and **Doubles**.

0 × 9	2 × 4	8 × 2	0 × 7	2 × 7	0 × 4	6 × 2

2 × 8	0 × 5	2 × 5	0 × 6	0 × 2	9 × 2	2 × 3

0 × 3	0 × 1	2 × 2	4 × 2	2 × 6	0 × 6	0 × 8

5 × 2	1 × 2	0 × 9	2 × 9	3 × 2	0 × 5	7 × 2

Cumulative Practice.

0 × 1	8 × 2	1 × 7	0 × 6	0 × 2	4 × 1	2 × 9

1 × 3	2 × 2	0 × 5	2 × 7	1 × 5	2 × 6	0 × 3

2 × 4	0 × 7	1 × 2	5 × 2	0 × 9	3 × 2	9 × 1

2 × 8	7 × 2	0 × 4	6 × 2	8 × 1	1 × 6	0 × 8

Name _____

More **Zero**

These answers are the same.

$\begin{array}{r} 0 \\ \times\,3 \\ \hline \end{array}$	$\begin{array}{r} 3 \\ \times\,0 \\ \hline \end{array}$
3 groups of 0 = 0	0 groups of 3 = 0

Practice **Zero** and **Doubles**.

$\begin{array}{r} 0 \\ \times\,6 \\ \hline \end{array}$ $\qquad$ $\begin{array}{r} 6 \\ \times\,0 \\ \hline \end{array}$ $\qquad$ $\begin{array}{r} 6 \\ \times\,2 \\ \hline \end{array}$ $\qquad$ $\begin{array}{r} 5 \\ \times\,0 \\ \hline \end{array}$ $\qquad$ $\begin{array}{r} 0 \\ \times\,8 \\ \hline \end{array}$ $\qquad$ $\begin{array}{r} 8 \\ \times\,2 \\ \hline \end{array}$ $\qquad$ $\begin{array}{r} 2 \\ \times\,0 \\ \hline \end{array}$

$\begin{array}{r} 3 \\ \times\,0 \\ \hline \end{array}$ $\qquad$ $\begin{array}{r} 2 \\ \times\,5 \\ \hline \end{array}$ $\qquad$ $\begin{array}{r} 9 \\ \times\,0 \\ \hline \end{array}$ $\qquad$ $\begin{array}{r} 2 \\ \times\,9 \\ \hline \end{array}$ $\qquad$ $\begin{array}{r} 7 \\ \times\,2 \\ \hline \end{array}$ $\qquad$ $\begin{array}{r} 0 \\ \times\,4 \\ \hline \end{array}$ $\qquad$ $\begin{array}{r} 7 \\ \times\,0 \\ \hline \end{array}$

$\begin{array}{r} 2 \\ \times\,4 \\ \hline \end{array}$ $\qquad$ $\begin{array}{r} 1 \\ \times\,0 \\ \hline \end{array}$ $\qquad$ $\begin{array}{r} 9 \\ \times\,2 \\ \hline \end{array}$ $\qquad$ $\begin{array}{r} 0 \\ \times\,9 \\ \hline \end{array}$ $\qquad$ $\begin{array}{r} 4 \\ \times\,0 \\ \hline \end{array}$ $\qquad$ $\begin{array}{r} 2 \\ \times\,3 \\ \hline \end{array}$ $\qquad$ $\begin{array}{r} 0 \\ \times\,5 \\ \hline \end{array}$

Practice with **Zero**. Watch +, −, and × signs.

$\begin{array}{r} 6 \\ \times\,0 \\ \hline \end{array}$ $\qquad$ $\begin{array}{r} 0 \\ \times\,7 \\ \hline \end{array}$ $\qquad$ $\begin{array}{r} 1 \\ -\,1 \\ \hline \end{array}$ $\qquad$ $\begin{array}{r} 6 \\ -\,0 \\ \hline \end{array}$ $\qquad$ $\begin{array}{r} 0 \\ \times\,3 \\ \hline \end{array}$ $\qquad$ $\begin{array}{r} 0 \\ +\,4 \\ \hline \end{array}$ $\qquad$ $\begin{array}{r} 7 \\ -\,7 \\ \hline \end{array}$

$\begin{array}{r} 5 \\ +\,0 \\ \hline \end{array}$ $\qquad$ $\begin{array}{r} 0 \\ +\,2 \\ \hline \end{array}$ $\qquad$ $\begin{array}{r} 0 \\ \times\,9 \\ \hline \end{array}$ $\qquad$ $\begin{array}{r} 6 \\ +\,0 \\ \hline \end{array}$ $\qquad$ $\begin{array}{r} 3 \\ -\,0 \\ \hline \end{array}$ $\qquad$ $\begin{array}{r} 5 \\ \times\,0 \\ \hline \end{array}$ $\qquad$ $\begin{array}{r} 0 \\ \times\,6 \\ \hline \end{array}$

$\begin{array}{r} 0 \\ \times\,4 \\ \hline \end{array}$ $\qquad$ $\begin{array}{r} 6 \\ -\,6 \\ \hline \end{array}$ $\qquad$ $\begin{array}{r} 8 \\ \times\,0 \\ \hline \end{array}$ $\qquad$ $\begin{array}{r} 1 \\ \times\,0 \\ \hline \end{array}$ $\qquad$ $\begin{array}{r} 0 \\ +\,9 \\ \hline \end{array}$ $\qquad$ $\begin{array}{r} 2 \\ \times\,0 \\ \hline \end{array}$ $\qquad$ $\begin{array}{r} 8 \\ -\,0 \\ \hline \end{array}$

Name _____

Practice **Zero** and **Doubles**.

3×0= _____	9×2= _____	5×0= _____	7×0= _____
2×4= _____	0×8= _____	2×7= _____	0×0= _____
4×0= _____	2×6= _____	2×0= _____	8×2= _____
5×2= _____	0×6= _____	3×2= _____	0×1= _____
0×9= _____	2×8= _____	0×3= _____	2×9= _____
2×3= _____	0×2= _____	6×2= _____	8×0= _____

Cumulative Practice.

0	2	5	1	2	0	8
× 9	× 8	× 0	× 2	× 6	× 6	× 1

9	7	2	1	5	2	0
× 2	× 0	× 2	× 7	× 1	× 3	× 1

1	2	8	0	8	6	0
× 9	× 4	× 2	× 3	× 0	× 1	× 2

1	1	4	5	3	9	2
× 4	× 1	× 0	× 2	× 1	× 0	× 7

Name _____

Count by 3s

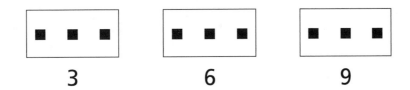

3   6   9

Three! Six! Nine! Who do you think is mighty fine?

$$\begin{array}{r} 3 \\ + 3 \\ \hline 6 \end{array}$$

$$\begin{array}{r} 6 \\ + 3 \\ \hline 9 \end{array}$$

3 groups of 3 = 9

(3+6=9 and 6+3=9)

3 × 3 = 9

Practice **Count by 3s** and **Doubles**. (Circle) **Count by 3s.**

$$\begin{array}{r} 3 \\ \times 3 \\ \hline \end{array}$$
$$\begin{array}{r} 4 \\ \times 2 \\ \hline \end{array}$$
$$\begin{array}{r} 2 \\ \times 6 \\ \hline \end{array}$$
$$\begin{array}{r} 3 \\ \times 3 \\ \hline \end{array}$$
$$\begin{array}{r} 2 \\ \times 2 \\ \hline \end{array}$$
$$\begin{array}{r} 2 \\ \times 3 \\ \hline \end{array}$$
$$\begin{array}{r} 3 \\ \times 3 \\ \hline \end{array}$$

$$\begin{array}{r} 8 \\ \times 2 \\ \hline \end{array}$$
$$\begin{array}{r} 2 \\ \times 5 \\ \hline \end{array}$$
$$\begin{array}{r} 3 \\ \times 3 \\ \hline \end{array}$$
$$\begin{array}{r} 9 \\ \times 2 \\ \hline \end{array}$$
$$\begin{array}{r} 6 \\ \times 2 \\ \hline \end{array}$$
$$\begin{array}{r} 3 \\ \times 3 \\ \hline \end{array}$$
$$\begin{array}{r} 2 \\ \times 7 \\ \hline \end{array}$$

$$\begin{array}{r} 2 \\ \times 2 \\ \hline \end{array}$$
$$\begin{array}{r} 3 \\ \times 3 \\ \hline \end{array}$$
$$\begin{array}{r} 7 \\ \times 2 \\ \hline \end{array}$$
$$\begin{array}{r} 2 \\ \times 8 \\ \hline \end{array}$$
$$\begin{array}{r} 3 \\ \times 3 \\ \hline \end{array}$$
$$\begin{array}{r} 2 \\ \times 9 \\ \hline \end{array}$$
$$\begin{array}{r} 3 \\ \times 2 \\ \hline \end{array}$$

$$\begin{array}{r} 3 \\ \times 3 \\ \hline \end{array}$$
$$\begin{array}{r} 2 \\ \times 9 \\ \hline \end{array}$$
$$\begin{array}{r} 8 \\ \times 2 \\ \hline \end{array}$$
$$\begin{array}{r} 2 \\ \times 4 \\ \hline \end{array}$$
$$\begin{array}{r} 5 \\ \times 2 \\ \hline \end{array}$$
$$\begin{array}{r} 3 \\ \times 3 \\ \hline \end{array}$$
$$\begin{array}{r} 4 \\ \times 2 \\ \hline \end{array}$$

Name _____

Practice **Count by 3s**, **1 Group**, and **Zero**.

3	0	5	3	1	0	1
× 3	× 2	× 0	× 3	× 3	× 3	× 5

1	3	4	6	3	1	3
× 2	× 3	× 1	× 0	× 3	× 9	× 3

7	0	3	0	3	3	1
× 1	× 9	× 3	× 4	× 0	× 3	× 8

3	1	1	3	1	7	0
× 3	× 1	× 0	× 3	× 6	× 0	× 8

Practice **Count by 3s** and **Doubles**.

3×3= _____   8×2= _____   2×3= _____   3×3= _____

2×5= _____   3×3= _____   2×2= _____   6×2= _____

4×2= _____   2×9= _____   3×3= _____   2×8= _____

3×3= _____   2×3= _____   5×2= _____   3×3= _____

2×7= _____   3×3= _____   2×4= _____   2×6= _____

3×2= _____   9×2= _____   3×3= _____   7×2= _____

Name _____

Practice **Count by 3s** with addition and subtraction.

3 × 3	6 + 3	9 − 3	3 × 3	9 − 6	3 × 3	3 + 6
9 − 6	3 × 3	3 + 6	9 − 3	3 + 3	6 + 3	3 × 3
9 − 3	6 + 3	3 × 3	3 + 6	3 × 3	9 − 6	3 + 3
3 + 6	3 × 3	9 − 6	3 + 3	9 − 3	3 × 3	6 + 3

Cumulative Practice.

3 × 3	2 × 0	1 × 9	8 × 2	0 × 8	3 × 3	4 × 1
9 × 0	1 × 3	3 × 3	2 × 5	3 × 3	0 × 5	2 × 3
7 × 2	3 × 3	0 × 4	2 × 2	2 × 9	6 × 1	3 × 3
1 × 8	4 × 2	1 × 5	3 × 3	2 × 6	3 × 3	6 × 0

Name _____

Cumulative Practice with addition and subtraction.

3 × 3	7 × 1	3 + 3	1 + 8	4 × 0	6 × 2	5 × 1
2 × 2	5 − 0	9 − 1	1 × 6	3 × 3	2 × 1	2 × 7
1 × 4	3 × 3	0 × 7	3 − 3	2 × 8	3 + 3	1 × 1
9 + 1	3 × 2	0 + 6	3 × 3	2 + 2	8 − 1	3 × 3

Practice this way.

2×5= _____	3×3= _____	1+3= _____	4×2= _____
3×0= _____	7×1= _____	9+9= _____	1×3= _____
3×3= _____	1+1= _____	7−1= _____	0+3= _____
1×9= _____	6−0= _____	3×3= _____	3+3= _____
8+0= _____	1−1= _____	4−1= _____	0×1= _____
2×9= _____	4+1= _____	9−0= _____	3×3= _____

Name _____

Count 5, 6, 7, 8

What is missing in the sequence?   ___, ___, **7, 8**

$$56 = 7 \times 8$$

Count 5, 6, 7, 8   8 ⟵
$$\begin{array}{r} 8 \\ \times\ 7 \\ \hline 56 \end{array}$$ groups of

This is the same. $$\begin{array}{r} 7 \\ \times\ 8 \\ \hline 56 \end{array}$$

Practice **Count 5, 6, 7, 8** and **1 Group**. (Circle) **Count 5, 6, 7, 8**.

$\begin{array}{r}8\\ \times\ 7\\ \hline\end{array}$	$\begin{array}{r}7\\ \times\ 1\\ \hline\end{array}$	$\begin{array}{r}7\\ \times\ 8\\ \hline\end{array}$	$\begin{array}{r}1\\ \times\ 8\\ \hline\end{array}$	$\begin{array}{r}7\\ \times\ 8\\ \hline\end{array}$	$\begin{array}{r}8\\ \times\ 1\\ \hline\end{array}$	$\begin{array}{r}8\\ \times\ 7\\ \hline\end{array}$
$\begin{array}{r}1\\ \times\ 8\\ \hline\end{array}$	$\begin{array}{r}7\\ \times\ 8\\ \hline\end{array}$	$\begin{array}{r}7\\ \times\ 1\\ \hline\end{array}$	$\begin{array}{r}7\\ \times\ 8\\ \hline\end{array}$	$\begin{array}{r}1\\ \times\ 8\\ \hline\end{array}$	$\begin{array}{r}8\\ \times\ 7\\ \hline\end{array}$	$\begin{array}{r}1\\ \times\ 7\\ \hline\end{array}$
$\begin{array}{r}7\\ \times\ 8\\ \hline\end{array}$	$\begin{array}{r}8\\ \times\ 1\\ \hline\end{array}$	$\begin{array}{r}8\\ \times\ 7\\ \hline\end{array}$	$\begin{array}{r}7\\ \times\ 1\\ \hline\end{array}$	$\begin{array}{r}8\\ \times\ 7\\ \hline\end{array}$	$\begin{array}{r}1\\ \times\ 7\\ \hline\end{array}$	$\begin{array}{r}7\\ \times\ 8\\ \hline\end{array}$

Practice **Count 5, 6, 7, 8** with addition and subtraction.

$\begin{array}{r}7\\ \times\ 8\\ \hline\end{array}$	$\begin{array}{r}8\\ +\ 7\\ \hline\end{array}$	$\begin{array}{r}8\\ \times\ 7\\ \hline\end{array}$	$\begin{array}{r}8\\ -\ 7\\ \hline\end{array}$	$\begin{array}{r}8\\ \times\ 7\\ \hline\end{array}$	$\begin{array}{r}7\\ \times\ 8\\ \hline\end{array}$	$\begin{array}{r}7\\ -\ 7\\ \hline\end{array}$
$\begin{array}{r}7\\ +\ 7\\ \hline\end{array}$	$\begin{array}{r}8\\ \times\ 7\\ \hline\end{array}$	$\begin{array}{r}7\\ \times\ 8\\ \hline\end{array}$	$\begin{array}{r}8\\ +\ 8\\ \hline\end{array}$	$\begin{array}{r}8\\ -\ 7\\ \hline\end{array}$	$\begin{array}{r}7\\ \times\ 8\\ \hline\end{array}$	$\begin{array}{r}7\\ +\ 8\\ \hline\end{array}$

Name _____

Practice **Count 5,6,7,8**, **Count by 3s**, and **Doubles**.

$\begin{array}{r}8\\ \times 7\\ \hline\end{array}$	$\begin{array}{r}2\\ \times 8\\ \hline\end{array}$	$\begin{array}{r}7\\ \times 8\\ \hline\end{array}$	$\begin{array}{r}3\\ \times 3\\ \hline\end{array}$	$\begin{array}{r}2\\ \times 4\\ \hline\end{array}$	$\begin{array}{r}8\\ \times 7\\ \hline\end{array}$	$\begin{array}{r}3\\ \times 3\\ \hline\end{array}$
$\begin{array}{r}3\\ \times 3\\ \hline\end{array}$	$\begin{array}{r}8\\ \times 7\\ \hline\end{array}$	$\begin{array}{r}2\\ \times 5\\ \hline\end{array}$	$\begin{array}{r}7\\ \times 8\\ \hline\end{array}$	$\begin{array}{r}3\\ \times 3\\ \hline\end{array}$	$\begin{array}{r}2\\ \times 2\\ \hline\end{array}$	$\begin{array}{r}7\\ \times 8\\ \hline\end{array}$
$\begin{array}{r}7\\ \times 2\\ \hline\end{array}$	$\begin{array}{r}2\\ \times 9\\ \hline\end{array}$	$\begin{array}{r}8\\ \times 7\\ \hline\end{array}$	$\begin{array}{r}3\\ \times 3\\ \hline\end{array}$	$\begin{array}{r}8\\ \times 7\\ \hline\end{array}$	$\begin{array}{r}3\\ \times 3\\ \hline\end{array}$	$\begin{array}{r}6\\ \times 2\\ \hline\end{array}$
$\begin{array}{r}7\\ \times 8\\ \hline\end{array}$	$\begin{array}{r}3\\ \times 3\\ \hline\end{array}$	$\begin{array}{r}9\\ \times 2\\ \hline\end{array}$	$\begin{array}{r}8\\ \times 7\\ \hline\end{array}$	$\begin{array}{r}3\\ \times 2\\ \hline\end{array}$	$\begin{array}{r}7\\ \times 8\\ \hline\end{array}$	$\begin{array}{r}3\\ \times 3\\ \hline\end{array}$

Practice **Count 5,6,7,8** and **Count by 3s** with addition and subtraction.

$8 \times 7 =$ _____	$3 \times 3 =$ _____	$7 \times 8 =$ _____	$3 + 3 =$ _____
$7 + 8 =$ _____	$8 - 7 =$ _____	$3 \times 3 =$ _____	$8 \times 7 =$ _____
$3 + 6 =$ _____	$7 \times 8 =$ _____	$9 - 6 =$ _____	$3 \times 3 =$ _____
$8 - 7 =$ _____	$3 \times 3 =$ _____	$7 \times 8 =$ _____	$6 + 3 =$ _____
$8 \times 7 =$ _____	$3 + 6 =$ _____	$8 + 7 =$ _____	$7 \times 8 =$ _____
$3 \times 3 =$ _____	$8 \times 7 =$ _____	$3 \times 3 =$ _____	$9 - 3 =$ _____

Name _____

Practice **Count 5, 6, 7, 8**, **1 Group**, and **Zero**.

7 × 8	8 × 0	8 × 7	1 × 1	1 × 7	0 × 6	7 × 8
0 × 1	8 × 7	8 × 1	0 × 7	1 × 4	7 × 8	1 × 9
6 × 1	2 × 1	7 × 0	7 × 8	0 × 3	1 × 5	8 × 7
5 × 0	7 × 8	3 × 1	2 × 0	8 × 7	9 × 0	0 × 4

Cumulative Practice.

8 × 7	4 × 1	5 × 2	3 × 3	8 × 7	9 × 1	2 × 8
0 × 8	7 × 8	1 × 6	4 × 2	3 × 0	9 × 2	7 × 8
2 × 2	2 × 7	7 × 8	4 × 0	3 × 3	8 × 7	1 × 8
7 × 1	0 × 5	3 × 2	2 × 6	7 × 8	1 × 5	8 × 7

Name _____

Cumulative Practice with addition and subtraction.

8 × 7	8 × 2	1 + 4	7 + 8	7 × 8	3 × 3	7 − 1
9 + 1	8 + 0	8 × 7	7 × 1	0 × 8	2 + 8	2 × 9
1 × 4	8 − 7	3 × 3	2 × 4	7 × 2	7 × 8	5 × 1
6 × 1	1 × 1	6 × 0	8 × 7	7 − 0	1 × 8	8 × 7
8 − 8	7 × 8	0 × 9	6 × 2	3 × 3	8 − 1	8 × 7
0 × 0	3 × 3	8 × 7	1 × 2	4 × 2	7 × 8	2 + 6
7 × 8	2 × 5	7 × 8	1 + 8	1 × 9	8 + 7	8 × 1
1 × 3	8 − 2	3 × 3	7 × 0	8 × 7	0 + 7	2 × 3

Name _____

I See 2 5s

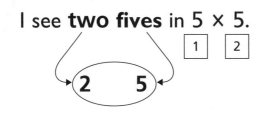 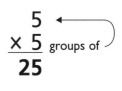

I see **two fives** in 5 × 5. 1 2

$$\begin{array}{r} 5 \\ \times\ 5 \\ \hline 25 \end{array}$$ groups of

Draw 5 groups of 5.

$$\begin{array}{r} 5 \\ \times\ 5 \\ \hline \end{array}$$ groups of

Remember this by saying, "I see 2 5s."

Practice **I See 2 5s**, **1 Group**, and **Count 5,6,7,8**.

5 × 5	5 × 1	5 × 5	1 × 5	8 × 7	5 × 5	1 × 7
7 × 8	5 × 5	8 × 1	7 × 8	5 × 5	5 × 1	8 × 7
1 × 5	8 × 7	1 × 7	5 × 5	1 × 8	7 × 8	5 × 5
7 × 8	5 × 1	5 × 5	7 × 1	8 × 7	5 × 5	7 × 8

Name _____

Practice **I See 2 5s**, **Count by 3s**, and **Doubles**.

5 × 5	4 × 2	3 × 3	2 × 6	5 × 5	8 × 2	2 × 5
2 × 3	3 × 3	5 × 5	7 × 2	2 × 2	5 × 5	3 × 3
9 × 2	5 × 5	5 × 2	3 × 2	3 × 3	1 × 2	5 × 5
5 × 5	2 × 8	3 × 3	5 × 5	6 × 2	3 × 3	2 × 9

Practice **I See 2 5s**, **Count 5,6,7,8**, and **Zero**.

$5 \times 5 =$ _____ $8 \times 7 =$ _____ $0 \times 8 =$ _____ $5 \times 5 =$ _____

$7 \times 0 =$ _____ $5 \times 5 =$ _____ $7 \times 8 =$ _____ $5 \times 0 =$ _____

$8 \times 7 =$ _____ $0 \times 5 =$ _____ $5 \times 5 =$ _____ $7 \times 8 =$ _____

$5 \times 5 =$ _____ $7 \times 8 =$ _____ $0 \times 7 =$ _____ $5 \times 5 =$ _____

$7 \times 8 =$ _____ $5 \times 5 =$ _____ $8 \times 0 =$ _____ $0 \times 5 =$ _____

$5 \times 0 =$ _____ $8 \times 7 =$ _____ $5 \times 5 =$ _____ $8 \times 7 =$ _____

Name _____

Practice **I See 2 5s** and **1 Group** with addition.

5	1	1	5	3	5	1
× 5	+ 8	× 6	× 5	+ 1	+ 5	× 5

9	5	1	1	5	1	5
× 1	× 5	× 4	+ 4	× 5	× 8	+ 1

5	1	7	5	2	1	5
+ 5	× 3	+ 1	× 5	× 1	× 7	× 5

1	1	5	6	1	5	2
× 1	+ 5	× 5	× 1	+ 1	× 1	+ 1

Cumulative Practice. (Circle) 5×5.

5	2	9	8	3	7	0
× 5	× 2	× 2	× 7	× 3	× 8	× 3

7	3	6	1	5	5	5
× 8	× 3	× 2	× 5	× 5	× 2	× 5

3	0	5	8	2	2	7
× 3	× 4	× 5	× 2	× 5	× 3	× 8

6	8	2	3	4	5	2
× 0	× 7	× 4	× 3	× 1	× 5	× 7

Name _____

Cumulative Practice with addition and subtraction.

$$\begin{array}{r} 7 \\ \times\ 2 \\ \hline \end{array} \qquad \begin{array}{r} 5 \\ \times\ 5 \\ \hline \end{array} \qquad \begin{array}{r} 1 \\ +\ 5 \\ \hline \end{array} \qquad \begin{array}{r} 5 \\ -\ 0 \\ \hline \end{array} \qquad \begin{array}{r} 4 \\ +\ 4 \\ \hline \end{array} \qquad \begin{array}{r} 9 \\ \times\ 1 \\ \hline \end{array} \qquad \begin{array}{r} 8 \\ \times\ 7 \\ \hline \end{array}$$

$$\begin{array}{r} 5 \\ -\ 5 \\ \hline \end{array} \qquad \begin{array}{r} 2 \\ \times\ 6 \\ \hline \end{array} \qquad \begin{array}{r} 3 \\ \times\ 3 \\ \hline \end{array} \qquad \begin{array}{r} 5 \\ \times\ 5 \\ \hline \end{array} \qquad \begin{array}{r} 4 \\ \times\ 2 \\ \hline \end{array} \qquad \begin{array}{r} 0 \\ \times\ 7 \\ \hline \end{array} \qquad \begin{array}{r} 8 \\ +\ 2 \\ \hline \end{array}$$

$$\begin{array}{r} 5 \\ \times\ 5 \\ \hline \end{array} \qquad \begin{array}{r} 2 \\ \times\ 0 \\ \hline \end{array} \qquad \begin{array}{r} 7 \\ +\ 7 \\ \hline \end{array} \qquad \begin{array}{r} 7 \\ \times\ 8 \\ \hline \end{array} \qquad \begin{array}{r} 5 \\ \times\ 5 \\ \hline \end{array} \qquad \begin{array}{r} 3 \\ +\ 1 \\ \hline \end{array} \qquad \begin{array}{r} 1 \\ \times\ 2 \\ \hline \end{array}$$

$$\begin{array}{r} 8 \\ \times\ 7 \\ \hline \end{array} \qquad \begin{array}{r} 9 \\ +\ 0 \\ \hline \end{array} \qquad \begin{array}{r} 5 \\ \times\ 5 \\ \hline \end{array} \qquad \begin{array}{r} 3 \\ -\ 1 \\ \hline \end{array} \qquad \begin{array}{r} 7 \\ \times\ 8 \\ \hline \end{array} \qquad \begin{array}{r} 5 \\ \times\ 5 \\ \hline \end{array} \qquad \begin{array}{r} 3 \\ \times\ 3 \\ \hline \end{array}$$

Practice this way.

$0 \times 3 =$ _____ $2 \times 3 =$ _____ $7 + 8 =$ _____ $5 \times 5 =$ _____

$2 + 4 =$ _____ $7 \times 1 =$ _____ $5 \times 2 =$ _____ $8 - 1 =$ _____

$5 \times 5 =$ _____ $7 - 7 =$ _____ $8 \times 7 =$ _____ $1 \times 1 =$ _____

$8 - 7 =$ _____ $5 \times 5 =$ _____ $2 - 0 =$ _____ $9 \times 2 =$ _____

$0 + 8 =$ _____ $1 \times 3 =$ _____ $1 + 1 =$ _____ $0 \times 9 =$ _____

$2 \times 8 =$ _____ $7 \times 8 =$ _____ $5 \times 5 =$ _____ $3 \times 3 =$ _____

Name _____

4 Fingers

6 + 6

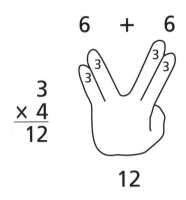

$$\begin{array}{r} 3 \\ \times\, 4 \\ \hline 12 \end{array}$$

12

4 groups of 3

⑥ + ⑥

―――――――――
12

Draw 3 groups of 4.

These are the same.

$$\begin{array}{r} 3 \\ \times\, \mathbf{4} \\ \hline 12 \end{array} \qquad \begin{array}{r} \mathbf{4} \\ \times\, 3 \\ \hline 12 \end{array}$$

Practice **4 Fingers**, **Count by 3s**, and **Count 5,6,7,8**. (Circle) 4.

④	8	3	4	3	4	7
× 3	× 7	× 4	× 3	× 3	× 3	× 8

7	3	8	3	4	8	3
× 8	× 4	× 7	× 3	× 3	× 7	× 4

3	7	4	3	8	3	3
× 3	× 8	× 3	× 4	× 7	× 4	× 3

8	4	3	7	3	7	3
× 7	× 3	× 3	× 8	× 4	× 8	× 4

Name _____

Practice **4 Fingers**, **I See 2 5s**, and **Zero**. (Circle) **4 Fingers**.

$$\begin{array}{r} 3 \\ \times\,4 \\ \hline \end{array} \qquad \begin{array}{r} 1 \\ \times\,0 \\ \hline \end{array} \qquad \begin{array}{r} 5 \\ \times\,5 \\ \hline \end{array} \qquad \begin{array}{r} 4 \\ \times\,3 \\ \hline \end{array} \qquad \begin{array}{r} 3 \\ \times\,4 \\ \hline \end{array} \qquad \begin{array}{r} 0 \\ \times\,9 \\ \hline \end{array} \qquad \begin{array}{r} 5 \\ \times\,5 \\ \hline \end{array}$$

$$\begin{array}{r} 3 \\ \times\,0 \\ \hline \end{array} \qquad \begin{array}{r} 4 \\ \times\,3 \\ \hline \end{array} \qquad \begin{array}{r} 7 \\ \times\,0 \\ \hline \end{array} \qquad \begin{array}{r} 5 \\ \times\,5 \\ \hline \end{array} \qquad \begin{array}{r} 0 \\ \times\,8 \\ \hline \end{array} \qquad \begin{array}{r} 3 \\ \times\,4 \\ \hline \end{array} \qquad \begin{array}{r} 0 \\ \times\,4 \\ \hline \end{array}$$

$$\begin{array}{r} 3 \\ \times\,4 \\ \hline \end{array} \qquad \begin{array}{r} 8 \\ \times\,0 \\ \hline \end{array} \qquad \begin{array}{r} 4 \\ \times\,3 \\ \hline \end{array} \qquad \begin{array}{r} 2 \\ \times\,0 \\ \hline \end{array} \qquad \begin{array}{r} 5 \\ \times\,5 \\ \hline \end{array} \qquad \begin{array}{r} 0 \\ \times\,6 \\ \hline \end{array} \qquad \begin{array}{r} 4 \\ \times\,3 \\ \hline \end{array}$$

$$\begin{array}{r} 5 \\ \times\,0 \\ \hline \end{array} \qquad \begin{array}{r} 3 \\ \times\,4 \\ \hline \end{array} \qquad \begin{array}{r} 5 \\ \times\,5 \\ \hline \end{array} \qquad \begin{array}{r} 0 \\ \times\,1 \\ \hline \end{array} \qquad \begin{array}{r} 0 \\ \times\,7 \\ \hline \end{array} \qquad \begin{array}{r} 4 \\ \times\,3 \\ \hline \end{array} \qquad \begin{array}{r} 0 \\ \times\,5 \\ \hline \end{array}$$

Practice **4 Fingers**, **Doubles**, and **1 Group**.

$$\begin{array}{r} 4 \\ \times\,3 \\ \hline \end{array} \qquad \begin{array}{r} 3 \\ \times\,1 \\ \hline \end{array} \qquad \begin{array}{r} 3 \\ \times\,4 \\ \hline \end{array} \qquad \begin{array}{r} 8 \\ \times\,2 \\ \hline \end{array} \qquad \begin{array}{r} 3 \\ \times\,2 \\ \hline \end{array} \qquad \begin{array}{r} 1 \\ \times\,4 \\ \hline \end{array} \qquad \begin{array}{r} 3 \\ \times\,4 \\ \hline \end{array}$$

$$\begin{array}{r} 2 \\ \times\,9 \\ \hline \end{array} \qquad \begin{array}{r} 3 \\ \times\,4 \\ \hline \end{array} \qquad \begin{array}{r} 6 \\ \times\,1 \\ \hline \end{array} \qquad \begin{array}{r} 4 \\ \times\,3 \\ \hline \end{array} \qquad \begin{array}{r} 1 \\ \times\,5 \\ \hline \end{array} \qquad \begin{array}{r} 4 \\ \times\,3 \\ \hline \end{array} \qquad \begin{array}{r} 1 \\ \times\,8 \\ \hline \end{array}$$

$$\begin{array}{r} 3 \\ \times\,4 \\ \hline \end{array} \qquad \begin{array}{r} 7 \\ \times\,2 \\ \hline \end{array} \qquad \begin{array}{r} 4 \\ \times\,3 \\ \hline \end{array} \qquad \begin{array}{r} 1 \\ \times\,1 \\ \hline \end{array} \qquad \begin{array}{r} 4 \\ \times\,3 \\ \hline \end{array} \qquad \begin{array}{r} 2 \\ \times\,6 \\ \hline \end{array} \qquad \begin{array}{r} 2 \\ \times\,2 \\ \hline \end{array}$$

$$\begin{array}{r} 7 \\ \times\,1 \\ \hline \end{array} \qquad \begin{array}{r} 4 \\ \times\,3 \\ \hline \end{array} \qquad \begin{array}{r} 1 \\ \times\,9 \\ \hline \end{array} \qquad \begin{array}{r} 2 \\ \times\,4 \\ \hline \end{array} \qquad \begin{array}{r} 2 \\ \times\,1 \\ \hline \end{array} \qquad \begin{array}{r} 3 \\ \times\,4 \\ \hline \end{array} \qquad \begin{array}{r} 2 \\ \times\,5 \\ \hline \end{array}$$

Name _____

Cumulative Practice.

4 × 3	2 × 2	5 × 5	3 × 3	3 × 4	1 × 2	8 × 7
8 × 7	0 × 4	3 × 4	1 × 6	2 × 3	4 × 3	2 × 5
9 × 1	4 × 3	7 × 8	5 × 5	9 × 2	3 × 3	3 × 4
5 × 5	6 × 2	1 × 1	3 × 4	0 × 3	8 × 7	4 × 1
3 × 4	1 × 3	5 × 5	7 × 8	4 × 3	9 × 0	5 × 1
5 × 2	3 × 4	1 × 0	5 × 5	7 × 8	3 × 3	4 × 3
3 × 3	7 × 8	4 × 3	2 × 7	5 × 5	2 × 8	1 × 7
2 × 0	4 × 3	4 × 2	8 × 7	3 × 4	0 × 0	3 × 3

Name _____

Cumulative Practice with addition and subtraction.

3 × 4	6 + 6	6 − 1	4 × 3	8 × 7	6 − 2	5 × 5
1 × 9	7 × 8	4 × 3	6 × 1	1 + 9	2 × 8	3 × 4
7 × 1	3 × 4	5 + 5	4 − 4	4 × 3	10 − 5	0 × 9
2 + 8	7 × 0	3 × 4	3 × 3	6 × 2	4 × 3	7 × 8
3 − 3	5 × 5	2 × 1	3 × 4	8 − 7	6 + 2	2 × 9
5 × 2	4 × 3	3 × 3	12 − 6	7 − 0	5 × 5	6 + 1
0 + 6	1 × 5	1 + 7	2 × 4	4 × 1	8 − 4	4 × 3
1 × 8	8 + 8	3 × 4	2 × 2	8 × 7	2 + 1	7 × 2

Five Times Five Is Not Ten: Make Multiplication Easy

Name _____

More 4 Fingers

8 + 8

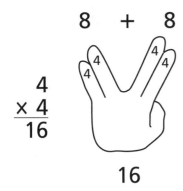

$$\begin{array}{r} 4 \\ \times\ 4 \\ \hline 16 \end{array}$$

16

4 groups of 4

⑧ + ⑧
_____
16

Practice **4 Fingers**.

$$\begin{array}{r}4\\ \times\ 4\\ \hline\end{array}\qquad \begin{array}{r}3\\ \times\ 4\\ \hline\end{array}\qquad \begin{array}{r}4\\ \times\ 4\\ \hline\end{array}\qquad \begin{array}{r}3\\ \times\ 4\\ \hline\end{array}\qquad \begin{array}{r}4\\ \times\ 3\\ \hline\end{array}\qquad \begin{array}{r}4\\ \times\ 4\\ \hline\end{array}\qquad \begin{array}{r}4\\ \times\ 3\\ \hline\end{array}$$

Practice **4 Fingers** and **Count by 3s** with addition.

$$\begin{array}{r}3\\ \times\ 4\\ \hline\end{array}\qquad \begin{array}{r}4\\ \times\ 4\\ \hline\end{array}\qquad \begin{array}{r}4\\ \times\ 3\\ \hline\end{array}\qquad \begin{array}{r}4\\ +\ 4\\ \hline\end{array}\qquad \begin{array}{r}4\\ \times\ 4\\ \hline\end{array}\qquad \begin{array}{r}3\\ \times\ 3\\ \hline\end{array}\qquad \begin{array}{r}4\\ +\ 3\\ \hline\end{array}$$

$$\begin{array}{r}4\\ \times\ 4\\ \hline\end{array}\qquad \begin{array}{r}3\\ +\ 3\\ \hline\end{array}\qquad \begin{array}{r}4\\ \times\ 4\\ \hline\end{array}\qquad \begin{array}{r}3\\ \times\ 4\\ \hline\end{array}\qquad \begin{array}{r}4\\ \times\ 3\\ \hline\end{array}\qquad \begin{array}{r}3\\ +\ 4\\ \hline\end{array}\qquad \begin{array}{r}3\\ \times\ 3\\ \hline\end{array}$$

$$\begin{array}{r}4\\ +\ 3\\ \hline\end{array}\qquad \begin{array}{r}3\\ \times\ 3\\ \hline\end{array}\qquad \begin{array}{r}3\\ \times\ 4\\ \hline\end{array}\qquad \begin{array}{r}4\\ \times\ 4\\ \hline\end{array}\qquad \begin{array}{r}3\\ +\ 4\\ \hline\end{array}\qquad \begin{array}{r}4\\ \times\ 4\\ \hline\end{array}\qquad \begin{array}{r}4\\ \times\ 3\\ \hline\end{array}$$

$$\begin{array}{r}4\\ \times\ 4\\ \hline\end{array}\qquad \begin{array}{r}4\\ \times\ 3\\ \hline\end{array}\qquad \begin{array}{r}4\\ +\ 4\\ \hline\end{array}\qquad \begin{array}{r}3\\ +\ 3\\ \hline\end{array}\qquad \begin{array}{r}3\\ \times\ 3\\ \hline\end{array}\qquad \begin{array}{r}3\\ \times\ 4\\ \hline\end{array}\qquad \begin{array}{r}4\\ \times\ 4\\ \hline\end{array}$$

Name _____

Practice **4 Fingers**, **1 Group**, and **I See 2 5s**.

3 × 4	4 × 4	7 × 1	5 × 5	9 × 1	4 × 4	4 × 3
1 × 8	5 × 5	4 × 4	5 × 1	4 × 3	1 × 6	4 × 4
4 × 3	3 × 4	3 × 1	4 × 4	1 × 2	5 × 5	1 × 4
4 × 4	1 × 7	5 × 5	4 × 1	4 × 4	3 × 4	5 × 5

Practice **4 Fingers**, **Zero**, and **Count by 3s**.

$4 \times 4 =$ _____ $9 \times 0 =$ _____ $3 \times 4 =$ _____ $3 \times 3 =$ _____

$0 \times 1 =$ _____ $4 \times 3 =$ _____ $4 \times 4 =$ _____ $3 \times 0 =$ _____

$3 \times 4 =$ _____ $3 \times 3 =$ _____ $0 \times 8 =$ _____ $3 \times 4 =$ _____

$4 \times 4 =$ _____ $7 \times 0 =$ _____ $4 \times 3 =$ _____ $4 \times 4 =$ _____

$3 \times 3 =$ _____ $3 \times 4 =$ _____ $4 \times 4 =$ _____ $3 \times 3 =$ _____

$0 \times 3 =$ _____ $4 \times 4 =$ _____ $4 \times 0 =$ _____ $4 \times 3 =$ _____

Name _____

Practice **4 Fingers**, **Zero**, and **Doubles**.

$$\begin{array}{r}4\\ \times\,3\\ \hline\end{array} \qquad \begin{array}{r}4\\ \times\,0\\ \hline\end{array} \qquad \begin{array}{r}6\\ \times\,2\\ \hline\end{array} \qquad \begin{array}{r}4\\ \times\,4\\ \hline\end{array} \qquad \begin{array}{r}2\\ \times\,9\\ \hline\end{array} \qquad \begin{array}{r}3\\ \times\,4\\ \hline\end{array} \qquad \begin{array}{r}0\\ \times\,3\\ \hline\end{array}$$

$$\begin{array}{r}8\\ \times\,2\\ \hline\end{array} \qquad \begin{array}{r}4\\ \times\,4\\ \hline\end{array} \qquad \begin{array}{r}4\\ \times\,3\\ \hline\end{array} \qquad \begin{array}{r}5\\ \times\,2\\ \hline\end{array} \qquad \begin{array}{r}0\\ \times\,6\\ \hline\end{array} \qquad \begin{array}{r}7\\ \times\,0\\ \hline\end{array} \qquad \begin{array}{r}3\\ \times\,4\\ \hline\end{array}$$

$$\begin{array}{r}4\\ \times\,4\\ \hline\end{array} \qquad \begin{array}{r}2\\ \times\,7\\ \hline\end{array} \qquad \begin{array}{r}0\\ \times\,5\\ \hline\end{array} \qquad \begin{array}{r}3\\ \times\,4\\ \hline\end{array} \qquad \begin{array}{r}4\\ \times\,3\\ \hline\end{array} \qquad \begin{array}{r}4\\ \times\,4\\ \hline\end{array} \qquad \begin{array}{r}2\\ \times\,3\\ \hline\end{array}$$

$$\begin{array}{r}2\\ \times\,0\\ \hline\end{array} \qquad \begin{array}{r}3\\ \times\,4\\ \hline\end{array} \qquad \begin{array}{r}2\\ \times\,4\\ \hline\end{array} \qquad \begin{array}{r}0\\ \times\,1\\ \hline\end{array} \qquad \begin{array}{r}4\\ \times\,4\\ \hline\end{array} \qquad \begin{array}{r}2\\ \times\,2\\ \hline\end{array} \qquad \begin{array}{r}4\\ \times\,3\\ \hline\end{array}$$

Practice **4 Fingers**, **I See 2 5s**, and **Count 5,6,7,8**.

4×4= _____   7×8= _____   3×4= _____   5×5= _____

8×7= _____   3×4= _____   5×5= _____   4×4= _____

4×3= _____   5×5= _____   8×7= _____   4×3= _____

3×4= _____   4×4= _____   4×3= _____   7×8= _____

4×4= _____   8×7= _____   5×5= _____   3×4= _____

7×8= _____   4×3= _____   4×4= _____   8×7= _____

Five Times Five Is Not Ten: Make Multiplication Easy **35**

Name _____

Cumulative Practice. (Circle) **4 Fingers**.

4 × 4	7 × 2	3 × 4	8 × 7	4 × 3	5 × 5	8 × 1
4 × 1	1 × 0	4 × 4	1 × 6	2 × 8	3 × 3	0 × 4
5 × 5	1 × 3	8 × 0	3 × 4	4 × 4	7 × 8	4 × 3
3 × 2	2 × 2	7 × 8	1 × 1	0 × 6	4 × 4	3 × 3
4 × 3	2 × 1	9 × 2	4 × 4	3 × 3	0 × 3	3 × 4
7 × 0	8 × 7	4 × 3	5 × 1	4 × 2	2 × 6	4 × 4
1 × 7	4 × 4	5 × 5	0 × 9	1 × 9	2 × 0	7 × 8
3 × 3	0 × 5	8 × 7	4 × 4	3 × 4	5 × 2	5 × 5

Five Times Five Is Not Ten: Make Multiplication Easy

Name _____

More **Count by 3s**

You know 3 × 3 = 9.

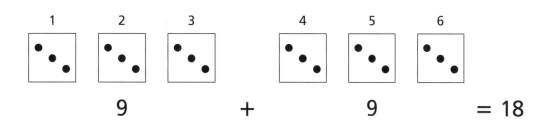

If 3 groups of 3 = 9,

then 6 groups of 3 = 18.

9   +   9   = 18

Learn 3×6=18 and 6×3=18.

Say, "Three! Six! Nine!   9 and 9 is 18."

Practice **Count by 3s**.

6	3	3	6	3	6	3
× 3	× 3	× 6	× 3	× 3	× 3	× 6

Practice **Count by 3s** and **I See 2 5s**.

3	5	6	3	6	5	3
× 6	× 5	× 3	× 3	× 3	× 5	× 3

5	6	3	3	5	3	6
× 5	× 3	× 3	× 6	× 5	× 3	× 3

Name _____

Practice **Count by 3s** and **Count 5,6,7,8**.

6 × 3	7 × 8	3 × 3	3 × 6	8 × 7	6 × 3	7 × 8
3 × 3	3 × 6	8 × 7	3 × 3	6 × 3	7 × 8	6 × 3
7 × 8	8 × 7	6 × 3	8 × 7	3 × 3	3 × 6	8 × 7
3 × 6	3 × 3	7 × 8	6 × 3	3 × 6	3 × 3	3 × 6

Practice **Count by 3s** and **1 Group**.

3 × 6	8 × 1	1 × 3	3 × 3	6 × 3	1 × 4	3 × 6
1 × 9	3 × 6	6 × 3	7 × 1	1 × 1	3 × 3	9 × 1
3 × 3	1 × 2	3 × 3	3 × 6	6 × 1	6 × 3	3 × 3
3 × 6	1 × 3	5 × 1	3 × 3	6 × 3	1 × 6	6 × 3

Name _____

Practice **Count by 3s** and **Doubles**.

3 × 6	3 × 3	7 × 2	2 × 5	6 × 3	2 × 4	6 × 3
2 × 8	6 × 3	3 × 2	3 × 6	2 × 2	3 × 6	6 × 2
9 × 2	2 × 6	3 × 3	6 × 3	2 × 3	2 × 7	3 × 6
3 × 3	4 × 2	3 × 6	8 × 2	3 × 3	6 × 3	5 × 2

Practice **Count by 3s**, **4 Fingers**, and **Zero**.

6 × 3	4 × 4	0 × 9	6 × 3	4 × 3	3 × 6	1 × 0
3 × 3	3 × 6	3 × 4	2 × 0	6 × 3	3 × 3	4 × 4
4 × 3	0 × 7	3 × 3	3 × 6	4 × 4	6 × 3	3 × 4
0 × 6	4 × 3	3 × 6	4 × 4	3 × 4	3 × 0	3 × 6

Name _____

Practice **Count by 3s** with addition and subtraction.

$3 \times 3 =$ _____ $3 \times 6 =$ _____ $6 + 3 =$ _____ $3 + 3 =$ _____

$6 \times 3 =$ _____ $3 + 6 =$ _____ $6 - 6 =$ _____ $3 \times 6 =$ _____

$0 + 3 =$ _____ $3 \times 3 =$ _____ $6 \times 3 =$ _____ $6 - 0 =$ _____

$3 \times 6 =$ _____ $6 - 3 =$ _____ $3 \times 3 =$ _____ $6 \times 3 =$ _____

$3 - 3 =$ _____ $6 \times 3 =$ _____ $3 + 3 =$ _____ $6 + 3 =$ _____

$3 + 6 =$ _____ $3 \times 6 =$ _____ $6 + 0 =$ _____ $3 - 0 =$ _____

Cumulative Practice.

6	1	8	3	4	6	3
$\times 3$	$\times 2$	$\times 7$	$\times 3$	$\times 3$	$\times 1$	$\times 6$

4	5	3	6	1	0	3
$\times 4$	$\times 5$	$\times 6$	$\times 2$	$\times 8$	$\times 5$	$\times 4$

9	4	6	6	7	2	3
$\times 1$	$\times 3$	$\times 0$	$\times 3$	$\times 8$	$\times 4$	$\times 3$

5	3	2	3	4	6	5
$\times 2$	$\times 6$	$\times 7$	$\times 4$	$\times 4$	$\times 3$	$\times 5$

Pretend to Add with 9

$$\begin{array}{r} 9 \\ \times\ 9 \\ \hline 81 \end{array}$$

Looks hard, so
Pretend to Add with 9

$$\begin{array}{r} 9 \\ +\ 9 \\ \hline \end{array}$$

to get the sound that starts **eight**een

$8 +\ \underline{\ ?\ }\ = 9$

$8 +\ \underline{\ 1\ }\ = 9$

$\boxed{81}$

$$\begin{array}{r} 9 \\ \times\ 9 \\ \hline 81 \end{array}$$

Draw 9 groups of 9.

Practice **Pretend to Add with 9** and **1 Group**. Circle $\begin{array}{r} 9 \\ \times\ 9 \end{array}$.

$\begin{array}{r}9\\\times\ 9\\\hline\end{array}$	$\begin{array}{r}9\\\times\ 1\\\hline\end{array}$	$\begin{array}{r}9\\\times\ 9\\\hline\end{array}$	$\begin{array}{r}1\\\times\ 3\\\hline\end{array}$	$\begin{array}{r}9\\\times\ 9\\\hline\end{array}$	$\begin{array}{r}5\\\times\ 1\\\hline\end{array}$	$\begin{array}{r}8\\\times\ 1\\\hline\end{array}$
$\begin{array}{r}4\\\times\ 1\\\hline\end{array}$	$\begin{array}{r}9\\\times\ 9\\\hline\end{array}$	$\begin{array}{r}6\\\times\ 1\\\hline\end{array}$	$\begin{array}{r}9\\\times\ 9\\\hline\end{array}$	$\begin{array}{r}1\\\times\ 7\\\hline\end{array}$	$\begin{array}{r}9\\\times\ 9\\\hline\end{array}$	$\begin{array}{r}1\\\times\ 6\\\hline\end{array}$
$\begin{array}{r}1\\\times\ 2\\\hline\end{array}$	$\begin{array}{r}7\\\times\ 1\\\hline\end{array}$	$\begin{array}{r}9\\\times\ 9\\\hline\end{array}$	$\begin{array}{r}1\\\times\ 9\\\hline\end{array}$	$\begin{array}{r}9\\\times\ 9\\\hline\end{array}$	$\begin{array}{r}1\\\times\ 4\\\hline\end{array}$	$\begin{array}{r}3\\\times\ 1\\\hline\end{array}$
$\begin{array}{r}9\\\times\ 9\\\hline\end{array}$	$\begin{array}{r}1\\\times\ 1\\\hline\end{array}$	$\begin{array}{r}1\\\times\ 8\\\hline\end{array}$	$\begin{array}{r}9\\\times\ 9\\\hline\end{array}$	$\begin{array}{r}1\\\times\ 5\\\hline\end{array}$	$\begin{array}{r}2\\\times\ 1\\\hline\end{array}$	$\begin{array}{r}9\\\times\ 9\\\hline\end{array}$

Name _____

Practice **Pretend to Add with 9** and **Count by 3s**.

$$\begin{array}{cc} 9 \\ \times\,9 \end{array}\qquad \begin{array}{cc} 3 \\ \times\,3 \end{array}\qquad \begin{array}{cc} 3 \\ \times\,6 \end{array}\qquad \begin{array}{cc} 9 \\ \times\,9 \end{array}\qquad \begin{array}{cc} 6 \\ \times\,3 \end{array}\qquad \begin{array}{cc} 9 \\ \times\,9 \end{array}\qquad \begin{array}{cc} 3 \\ \times\,3 \end{array}$$

$$\begin{array}{cc} 6 \\ \times\,3 \end{array}\qquad \begin{array}{cc} 9 \\ \times\,9 \end{array}\qquad \begin{array}{cc} 3 \\ \times\,3 \end{array}\qquad \begin{array}{cc} 3 \\ \times\,6 \end{array}\qquad \begin{array}{cc} 9 \\ \times\,9 \end{array}\qquad \begin{array}{cc} 3 \\ \times\,3 \end{array}\qquad \begin{array}{cc} 6 \\ \times\,3 \end{array}$$

$$\begin{array}{cc} 3 \\ \times\,3 \end{array}\qquad \begin{array}{cc} 3 \\ \times\,6 \end{array}\qquad \begin{array}{cc} 9 \\ \times\,9 \end{array}\qquad \begin{array}{cc} 3 \\ \times\,3 \end{array}\qquad \begin{array}{cc} 3 \\ \times\,6 \end{array}\qquad \begin{array}{cc} 6 \\ \times\,3 \end{array}\qquad \begin{array}{cc} 9 \\ \times\,9 \end{array}$$

$$\begin{array}{cc} 3 \\ \times\,6 \end{array}\qquad \begin{array}{cc} 9 \\ \times\,9 \end{array}\qquad \begin{array}{cc} 6 \\ \times\,3 \end{array}\qquad \begin{array}{cc} 9 \\ \times\,9 \end{array}\qquad \begin{array}{cc} 3 \\ \times\,3 \end{array}\qquad \begin{array}{cc} 9 \\ \times\,9 \end{array}\qquad \begin{array}{cc} 3 \\ \times\,6 \end{array}$$

Practice **Pretend to Add with 9**, **I See 2 5s**, and **Zero**.

$9 \times 9 =$ _____ $0 \times 9 =$ _____ $2 \times 0 =$ _____ $9 \times 9 =$ _____

$0 \times 5 =$ _____ $5 \times 5 =$ _____ $9 \times 9 =$ _____ $7 \times 0 =$ _____

$5 \times 5 =$ _____ $4 \times 0 =$ _____ $0 \times 3 =$ _____ $5 \times 5 =$ _____

$9 \times 0 =$ _____ $9 \times 9 =$ _____ $5 \times 5 =$ _____ $0 \times 1 =$ _____

$8 \times 0 =$ _____ $5 \times 5 =$ _____ $0 \times 6 =$ _____ $9 \times 9 =$ _____

$5 \times 5 =$ _____ $5 \times 0 =$ _____ $9 \times 9 =$ _____ $5 \times 5 =$ _____

Name _____

Practice **Pretend to Add with 9**, **I See 2 5s**, and **Doubles**.

9	5	5	9	7	2	2
× 9	× 2	× 5	× 9	× 2	× 2	× 3

5	2	9	5	2	2	9
× 5	× 8	× 9	× 5	× 6	× 9	× 9

4	9	9	9	5	9	2
× 2	× 9	× 2	× 9	× 5	× 9	× 5

9	5	6	2	9	8	5
× 9	× 5	× 2	× 7	× 9	× 2	× 5

Practice **Pretend to Add with 9**, **4 Fingers**, and **Count 5,6,7,8**.

9	8	3	7	4	9	4
× 9	× 7	× 4	× 8	× 4	× 9	× 3

7	4	4	9	3	8	4
× 8	× 3	× 4	× 9	× 4	× 7	× 4

3	8	9	4	9	4	9
× 4	× 7	× 9	× 4	× 9	× 3	× 9

8	9	7	4	4	7	3
× 7	× 9	× 8	× 3	× 4	× 8	× 4

Name _____

Cumulative Practice.

9 × 9	2 × 5	8 × 7	4 × 3	9 × 1	3 × 6	3 × 3
9 × 2	5 × 5	4 × 0	9 × 9	4 × 4	9 × 9	7 × 8
6 × 3	9 × 9	1 × 5	3 × 2	3 × 6	2 × 8	9 × 9
3 × 4	7 × 8	9 × 9	1 × 1	9 × 9	8 × 0	6 × 3
9 × 9	4 × 2	3 × 6	1 × 6	2 × 9	9 × 9	4 × 1
8 × 7	4 × 3	5 × 5	9 × 9	2 × 2	7 × 1	3 × 4
1 × 8	9 × 9	0 × 3	2 × 1	3 × 6	1 × 3	2 × 6
7 × 2	6 × 3	9 × 9	4 × 4	8 × 7	3 × 3	0 × 5

More Pretend to Add with 9

$$\begin{array}{r} 9 \\ \times\,7 \\ \hline 63 \end{array}$$

Looks hard, so
Pretend to Add with 9

$$\begin{array}{r} 9 \\ +\,7 \\ \hline \end{array}$$

to get the sound that starts **six**teen

6 + ? = 9

6 + 3 = 9

63

These are the same.

$\begin{array}{r} 9 \\ \times\,7 \\ \hline 63 \end{array}$	$\begin{array}{r} 7 \\ \times\,9 \\ \hline 63 \end{array}$

Practice **Pretend to Add with 9** and **Doubles**. (Circle) **Pretend to Add with 9**.

$\begin{array}{r} 7 \\ \times\,9 \\ \hline \end{array}$	$\begin{array}{r} 3 \\ \times\,2 \\ \hline \end{array}$	$\begin{array}{r} 9 \\ \times\,7 \\ \hline \end{array}$	$\begin{array}{r} 2 \\ \times\,4 \\ \hline \end{array}$	$\begin{array}{r} 7 \\ \times\,9 \\ \hline \end{array}$	$\begin{array}{r} 9 \\ \times\,9 \\ \hline \end{array}$	$\begin{array}{r} 8 \\ \times\,2 \\ \hline \end{array}$
$\begin{array}{r} 6 \\ \times\,2 \\ \hline \end{array}$	$\begin{array}{r} 9 \\ \times\,7 \\ \hline \end{array}$	$\begin{array}{r} 5 \\ \times\,2 \\ \hline \end{array}$	$\begin{array}{r} 7 \\ \times\,9 \\ \hline \end{array}$	$\begin{array}{r} 9 \\ \times\,9 \\ \hline \end{array}$	$\begin{array}{r} 2 \\ \times\,7 \\ \hline \end{array}$	$\begin{array}{r} 9 \\ \times\,7 \\ \hline \end{array}$
$\begin{array}{r} 9 \\ \times\,9 \\ \hline \end{array}$	$\begin{array}{r} 2 \\ \times\,8 \\ \hline \end{array}$	$\begin{array}{r} 7 \\ \times\,9 \\ \hline \end{array}$	$\begin{array}{r} 2 \\ \times\,9 \\ \hline \end{array}$	$\begin{array}{r} 4 \\ \times\,2 \\ \hline \end{array}$	$\begin{array}{r} 9 \\ \times\,7 \\ \hline \end{array}$	$\begin{array}{r} 9 \\ \times\,9 \\ \hline \end{array}$
$\begin{array}{r} 2 \\ \times\,3 \\ \hline \end{array}$	$\begin{array}{r} 7 \\ \times\,9 \\ \hline \end{array}$	$\begin{array}{r} 9 \\ \times\,9 \\ \hline \end{array}$	$\begin{array}{r} 9 \\ \times\,7 \\ \hline \end{array}$	$\begin{array}{r} 7 \\ \times\,2 \\ \hline \end{array}$	$\begin{array}{r} 9 \\ \times\,9 \\ \hline \end{array}$	$\begin{array}{r} 2 \\ \times\,2 \\ \hline \end{array}$

Name _____

Practice **Pretend to Add with 9** and **4 Fingers**.

7	9	4	3	9	4	7
× 9	× 9	× 4	× 4	× 7	× 3	× 9

3	9	4	9	3	7	4
× 4	× 7	× 3	× 9	× 4	× 9	× 4

9	4	7	4	9	3	9
× 9	× 3	× 9	× 4	× 7	× 4	× 7

4	7	9	4	4	9	9
× 4	× 9	× 9	× 3	× 4	× 7	× 9

Practice **Pretend to Add with 9** with addition.

9×7= _____   7+9= _____   9×9= _____   9×7= _____

7+7= _____   9×7= _____   7×9= _____   9+9= _____

7×9= _____   9+7= _____   9+9= _____   9×9= _____

9×7= _____   9×9= _____   7+9= _____   7×9= _____

9+7= _____   7×9= _____   9×9= _____   9×7= _____

9×9= _____   7+7= _____   9×7= _____   9×9= _____

Name _____

Practice **Pretend to Add with 9**, **Count 5,6,7,8**, and **1 Group**.

9 × 7	9 × 9	3 × 1	8 × 7	1 × 9	7 × 9	7 × 8
1 × 8	8 × 7	9 × 7	7 × 1	7 × 8	1 × 6	9 × 7
7 × 9	2 × 1	7 × 8	9 × 7	5 × 1	8 × 7	9 × 9
7 × 8	7 × 9	9 × 9	1 × 4	7 × 9	1 × 1	8 × 7

Practice **Pretend to Add with 9**, **Count by 3s**, and **I See 2 5s**.

9 × 9	3 × 3	9 × 7	3 × 6	7 × 9	5 × 5	6 × 3
5 × 5	6 × 3	9 × 9	9 × 7	3 × 3	3 × 6	7 × 9
6 × 3	9 × 7	5 × 5	9 × 9	3 × 6	7 × 9	3 × 3
7 × 9	3 × 3	3 × 6	9 × 7	5 × 5	6 × 3	9 × 9

Five Times Five Is Not Ten: Make Multiplication Easy **47**

Name _____

Practice **Pretend to Add with 9** with subtraction.

7×9= _____	7−1= _____	9−7= _____	9×7= _____
9−0= _____	7×9= _____	9×9= _____	9−9= _____
9×7= _____	8−4= _____	9×7= _____	10−1= _____
9×9= _____	7−7= _____	18−9= _____	5−1= _____
6−3= _____	9×7= _____	7−0= _____	9×9= _____
7×9= _____	9×9= _____	9×7= _____	9−1= _____

Cumulative Practice.

8 × 2	9 × 7	3 × 2	5 × 5	7 × 9	4 × 3	2 × 5
9 × 9	3 × 3	8 × 7	5 × 1	6 × 3	8 × 0	9 × 7
0 × 4	6 × 2	7 × 9	3 × 4	2 × 4	7 × 8	9 × 9
3 × 6	4 × 4	2 × 9	9 × 7	2 × 7	1 × 7	7 × 9

More **Pretend to Add with 9**

$$\begin{array}{r} 9 \\ \times\ 4 \\ \hline 36 \end{array}$$

Looks hard, so
Pretend to Add with 9

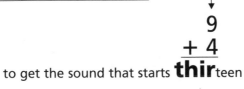

$$\begin{array}{r} 9 \\ +\ 4 \end{array}$$

to get the sound that starts **thir**teen

3 + _?_ = 9

3 + **6** = 9

(36)

9 groups of 4

$$\begin{array}{r} 4 \\ \times\ 9 \\ \hline 36 \end{array}$$

| 4 | 4 | 4 | | 4 | 4 | 4 | | 4 | 4 | 4 |

12   +   12   +   12

$$\begin{array}{r} 12 \\ 12 \\ +\ 12 \\ \hline 36 \end{array}$$

These are the same.

$$\begin{array}{r} 9 \\ \times\ 4 \\ \hline \mathbf{36} \end{array} \qquad \begin{array}{r} 4 \\ \times\ 9 \\ \hline \mathbf{36} \end{array}$$

(This is also **4 Fingers**. 4×9= 4 groups of 9. (9+9) and (9+9)=18+18=36.)

Practice **Pretend to Add with 9**.

$$\begin{array}{r} 4 \\ \times\ 9 \\ \hline \end{array} \quad \begin{array}{r} 9 \\ \times\ 4 \\ \hline \end{array} \quad \begin{array}{r} 7 \\ \times\ 9 \\ \hline \end{array} \quad \begin{array}{r} 9 \\ \times\ 4 \\ \hline \end{array} \quad \begin{array}{r} 9 \\ \times\ 9 \\ \hline \end{array} \quad \begin{array}{r} 4 \\ \times\ 9 \\ \hline \end{array} \quad \begin{array}{r} 9 \\ \times\ 7 \\ \hline \end{array}$$

$$\begin{array}{r} 9 \\ \times\ 4 \\ \hline \end{array} \quad \begin{array}{r} 9 \\ \times\ 7 \\ \hline \end{array} \quad \begin{array}{r} 4 \\ \times\ 9 \\ \hline \end{array} \quad \begin{array}{r} 9 \\ \times\ 9 \\ \hline \end{array} \quad \begin{array}{r} 9 \\ \times\ 4 \\ \hline \end{array} \quad \begin{array}{r} 7 \\ \times\ 9 \\ \hline \end{array} \quad \begin{array}{r} 4 \\ \times\ 9 \\ \hline \end{array}$$

$$\begin{array}{r} 7 \\ \times\ 9 \\ \hline \end{array} \quad \begin{array}{r} 9 \\ \times\ 9 \\ \hline \end{array} \quad \begin{array}{r} 9 \\ \times\ 7 \\ \hline \end{array} \quad \begin{array}{r} 4 \\ \times\ 9 \\ \hline \end{array} \quad \begin{array}{r} 9 \\ \times\ 7 \\ \hline \end{array} \quad \begin{array}{r} 9 \\ \times\ 4 \\ \hline \end{array} \quad \begin{array}{r} 7 \\ \times\ 9 \\ \hline \end{array}$$

Name _____

Practice **Pretend to Add with 9** and **Count by 3s**.

9 × 4	9 × 7	3 × 3	4 × 9	3 × 6	9 × 9	7 × 9
3 × 6	4 × 9	7 × 9	6 × 3	3 × 3	9 × 4	9 × 9
9 × 7	6 × 3	9 × 4	3 × 3	7 × 9	6 × 3	4 × 9
9 × 9	9 × 4	3 × 6	9 × 9	4 × 9	9 × 7	3 × 3

Practice **Pretend to Add with 9** and **Doubles**.

7 × 9	9 × 4	4 × 2	9 × 7	9 × 9	2 × 2	7 × 9
9 × 9	2 × 8	7 × 9	4 × 9	7 × 2	9 × 7	9 × 4
2 × 9	9 × 7	9 × 9	4 × 9	2 × 3	9 × 4	2 × 6
4 × 9	5 × 2	9 × 4	9 × 2	9 × 7	9 × 9	4 × 9

Five Times Five Is Not Ten: Make Multiplication Easy

Name _____

Practice **Pretend to Add with 9**, **Count 5,6,7,8**, and **I See 2 5s**.

9 × 9	8 × 7	7 × 9	5 × 5	4 × 9	7 × 8	9 × 4
7 × 9	5 × 5	9 × 4	9 × 7	8 × 7	4 × 9	7 × 8
7 × 8	9 × 4	9 × 7	4 × 9	5 × 5	8 × 7	9 × 9
5 × 5	7 × 9	7 × 8	8 × 7	9 × 4	9 × 7	4 × 9

Practice **Pretend to Add with 9**, **Zero**, and **4 Fingers**.

4 × 9	9 × 9	7 × 9	3 × 4	9 × 4	4 × 4	0 × 9
9 × 7	4 × 3	3 × 0	9 × 7	9 × 9	0 × 6	9 × 4
7 × 0	9 × 7	4 × 4	0 × 5	4 × 9	4 × 3	4 × 0
3 × 4	0 × 1	9 × 4	7 × 9	8 × 0	4 × 9	9 × 7

Name _____

Cumulative Practice.

9 × 7	2 × 8	9 × 2	4 × 4	9 × 9	4 × 9	4 × 3
9 × 0	7 × 8	5 × 5	7 × 9	3 × 4	6 × 1	3 × 3
9 × 4	2 × 7	1 × 4	9 × 4	3 × 6	4 × 3	9 × 7
4 × 4	5 × 2	6 × 3	3 × 4	4 × 9	8 × 7	0 × 7
9 × 7	3 × 6	3 × 4	5 × 1	9 × 9	4 × 4	4 × 2
8 × 7	9 × 4	5 × 5	0 × 2	2 × 6	3 × 6	2 × 2
3 × 2	7 × 9	4 × 3	4 × 9	7 × 2	1 × 1	4 × 4
6 × 3	1 × 9	7 × 8	2 × 9	3 × 3	8 × 1	7 × 9

Rhymes

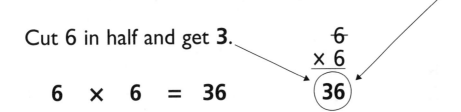

Six times six is thirty-six.

Cut 6 in half and get **3**.

6 × 6 = 36

$$\begin{array}{r} 6 \\ \times\ 6 \\ \hline (36) \end{array}$$

Practice **Rhymes** with addition and subtraction.

6×6= _____	6−1= _____	6×6= _____	6+6= _____
12−6= _____	6+6= _____	1+6= _____	6×6= _____
6+0= _____	6×6= _____	6−0= _____	0+6= _____
6×6= _____	6−6= _____	12−6= _____	6×6= _____

Practice **Rhymes**, **1 Group**, and **Zero**.

6 × 6	1 × 7	1 × 0	6 × 6	9 × 1	0 × 4	6 × 6
1 × 6	6 × 6	0 × 6	8 × 0	6 × 6	3 × 1	6 × 0
5 × 0	6 × 1	6 × 6	1 × 8	0 × 7	6 × 6	2 × 1

Name _____

Practice **Rhymes** and **4 Fingers**.

6 × 6	4 × 4	6 × 6	4 × 3	6 × 6	4 × 4	6 × 6
3 × 4	6 × 6	4 × 3	4 × 4	4 × 3	6 × 6	3 × 4
6 × 6	3 × 4	4 × 4	6 × 6	3 × 4	4 × 3	6 × 6
4 × 4	6 × 6	4 × 3	4 × 4	6 × 6	3 × 4	4 × 4

Practice **Rhymes**, **Count by 3s**, and **Count 5,6,7,8**.

6 × 6	8 × 7	3 × 3	6 × 6	3 × 6	7 × 8	6 × 6
6 × 3	6 × 6	7 × 8	3 × 6	6 × 6	3 × 3	6 × 3
8 × 7	3 × 3	6 × 6	8 × 7	6 × 3	6 × 6	7 × 8
3 × 6	6 × 6	6 × 3	3 × 3	7 × 8	3 × 6	8 × 7

Name _____

Practice **Rhymes** and **Pretend to Add with 9**.

6 × 6	9 × 7	7 × 9	9 × 4	6 × 6	7 × 9	4 × 9
9 × 9	6 × 6	9 × 4	7 × 9	4 × 9	6 × 6	9 × 9
9 × 4	9 × 9	6 × 6	4 × 9	6 × 6	9 × 7	6 × 6
7 × 9	4 × 9	9 × 7	6 × 6	9 × 4	6 × 6	9 × 7

Practice **Rhymes**, **I See 2 5s**, and **Doubles**.

6 × 6	5 × 5	6 × 2	2 × 7	2 × 3	6 × 6	2 × 8
5 × 5	4 × 2	6 × 6	5 × 2	6 × 6	2 × 2	5 × 5
2 × 9	6 × 6	5 × 5	6 × 6	9 × 2	5 × 5	2 × 5
6 × 6	8 × 2	2 × 4	5 × 5	2 × 6	7 × 2	6 × 6

Name _____

Cumulative Practice.

7	6	3	7	1	6	7
× 9	× 6	× 4	× 2	× 8	× 6	× 8

7	3	6	9	3	0	4
× 1	× 3	× 6	× 4	× 6	× 5	× 3

5	4	2	9	6	8	4
× 5	× 4	× 2	× 7	× 6	× 7	× 1

6	2	6	1	4	6	9
× 6	× 8	× 3	× 5	× 9	× 6	× 9

Practice this way.

$9 \times 1 =$ _____ $6 \times 6 =$ _____ $0 \times 9 =$ _____ $4 \times 9 =$ _____

$4 \times 3 =$ _____ $5 \times 5 =$ _____ $1 \times 6 =$ _____ $6 \times 6 =$ _____

$8 \times 7 =$ _____ $6 \times 3 =$ _____ $7 \times 9 =$ _____ $2 \times 6 =$ _____

$6 \times 6 =$ _____ $9 \times 9 =$ _____ $3 \times 3 =$ _____ $7 \times 8 =$ _____

$9 \times 2 =$ _____ $6 \times 6 =$ _____ $4 \times 2 =$ _____ $3 \times 6 =$ _____

$9 \times 7 =$ _____ $9 \times 4 =$ _____ $4 \times 4 =$ _____ $3 \times 4 =$ _____

More **Rhymes**

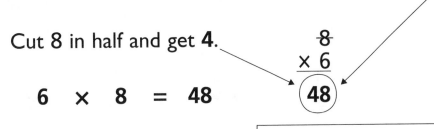

Six times eight is forty-eight.

Cut 8 in half and get **4**.

$$6 \times 8 = 48$$

$$\begin{array}{r} \cancel{8} \\ \times\,6 \\ \hline \end{array}$$
$\boxed{48}$

These are the same.

8	6
× **6**	× **8**
48	48

You know 2 × 6 = 12.

8 groups of 6 = 48

12	+	12	+	12	+	12

| 6 | 6 | | 6 | 6 | | 6 | 6 | | 6 | 6 |

12+12=24   and   12+12=24

$$\begin{array}{r} 24 \\ +\,24 \\ \hline \mathbf{48} \end{array}$$

Practice **Rhymes**, **I See 2 5s**, and **Zero**.

$\begin{array}{r}8\\\times\,6\\\hline\end{array}$	$\begin{array}{r}8\\\times\,0\\\hline\end{array}$	$\begin{array}{r}5\\\times\,5\\\hline\end{array}$	$\begin{array}{r}6\\\times\,8\\\hline\end{array}$	$\begin{array}{r}6\\\times\,6\\\hline\end{array}$	$\begin{array}{r}6\\\times\,8\\\hline\end{array}$	$\begin{array}{r}0\\\times\,6\\\hline\end{array}$
$\begin{array}{r}6\\\times\,8\\\hline\end{array}$	$\begin{array}{r}5\\\times\,5\\\hline\end{array}$	$\begin{array}{r}6\\\times\,6\\\hline\end{array}$	$\begin{array}{r}0\\\times\,5\\\hline\end{array}$	$\begin{array}{r}8\\\times\,6\\\hline\end{array}$	$\begin{array}{r}6\\\times\,6\\\hline\end{array}$	$\begin{array}{r}5\\\times\,5\\\hline\end{array}$
$\begin{array}{r}6\\\times\,0\\\hline\end{array}$	$\begin{array}{r}8\\\times\,6\\\hline\end{array}$	$\begin{array}{r}0\\\times\,8\\\hline\end{array}$	$\begin{array}{r}6\\\times\,6\\\hline\end{array}$	$\begin{array}{r}5\\\times\,0\\\hline\end{array}$	$\begin{array}{r}5\\\times\,5\\\hline\end{array}$	$\begin{array}{r}6\\\times\,8\\\hline\end{array}$

Name _____

Practice **Rhymes**, **1 Group**, and **4 Fingers**.

8 × 6	4 × 1	4 × 4	6 × 8	3 × 4	6 × 6	1 × 8
6 × 6	8 × 6	1 × 9	4 × 3	6 × 8	7 × 1	4 × 4
1 × 6	1 × 1	3 × 4	8 × 6	3 × 1	6 × 8	6 × 6
4 × 3	6 × 8	2 × 1	6 × 6	4 × 4	3 × 4	8 × 6

Practice **Rhymes** and **Doubles**.

6 × 8	8 × 2	6 × 6	2 × 6	8 × 6	9 × 2	6 × 8
7 × 2	6 × 6	6 × 8	2 × 3	6 × 6	8 × 6	2 × 8
5 × 2	8 × 6	2 × 4	6 × 8	2 × 2	6 × 6	6 × 8
6 × 6	2 × 9	8 × 6	2 × 7	8 × 6	6 × 2	2 × 5

Name _____

Practice **Rhymes** and <u>Count by 3s</u>.

6 × 6	8 × 6	3 × 3	3 × 6	3 × 3	8 × 6	6 × 8
6 × 3	6 × 6	6 × 8	3 × 3	8 × 6	3 × 6	6 × 3
6 × 8	3 × 3	3 × 6	6 × 8	6 × 3	6 × 6	8 × 6
3 × 6	8 × 6	6 × 6	6 × 3	6 × 8	3 × 3	6 × 6

Practice **Rhymes** and <u>**Pretend to Add with 9**</u>.

$6 \times 8 =$ _____ $9 \times 7 =$ _____ $8 \times 6 =$ _____ $9 \times 4 =$ _____

$9 \times 9 =$ _____ $6 \times 6 =$ _____ $4 \times 9 =$ _____ $6 \times 8 =$ _____

$9 \times 7 =$ _____ $9 \times 9 =$ _____ $7 \times 9 =$ _____ $6 \times 6 =$ _____

$8 \times 6 =$ _____ $9 \times 4 =$ _____ $6 \times 8 =$ _____ $9 \times 7 =$ _____

$6 \times 6 =$ _____ $6 \times 8 =$ _____ $8 \times 6 =$ _____ $4 \times 9 =$ _____

$7 \times 9 =$ _____ $6 \times 6 =$ _____ $9 \times 9 =$ _____ $8 \times 6 =$ _____

Name _____

Practice **Rhymes** and **Count 5,6,7,8** with addition.

8 × 6	8 + 0	6 × 8	6 + 6	8 × 7	7 + 8	6 × 6
7 + 7	6 + 8	8 × 7	6 × 8	0 + 6	8 × 6	7 × 8
6 × 6	7 + 0	8 × 6	8 + 7	7 × 8	6 × 6	8 × 6
7 × 8	6 × 8	8 + 8	8 × 7	0 + 8	6 × 8	8 + 6

Cumulative Practice.

6 × 8	1 × 3	5 × 5	2 × 8	3 × 4	8 × 6	4 × 9
9 × 7	3 × 3	8 × 6	3 × 6	2 × 5	4 × 4	2 × 0
6 × 3	7 × 2	7 × 9	6 × 0	8 × 7	5 × 1	2 × 3
6 × 6	9 × 4	6 × 2	9 × 9	6 × 8	4 × 3	7 × 8

Five Times Five Is Not Ten: Make Multiplication Easy

Fives

Count the dots in 3 groups of 5.

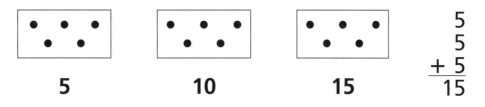

5	**10**	**15**	5 5 + 5 15

These are the same.

$$\begin{array}{cc} 5 & 3 \\ \times\ 3 & \times\ 5 \\ \hline \textbf{15} & \textbf{15} \end{array}$$

Draw $\begin{array}{c} 3 \\ \times\ 5 \end{array}$ groups of

Remember that 3×5 and 5×3=15.

Practice **Fives** and **Rhymes**. Circle **Fives**.

5 × 3	6 × 6	8 × 6	3 × 5	5 × 3	8 × 6	6 × 6
6 × 8	3 × 5	6 × 6	5 × 3	6 × 8	3 × 5	8 × 6
6 × 6	8 × 6	3 × 5	6 × 8	5 × 3	6 × 6	5 × 3
3 × 5	6 × 6	6 × 8	5 × 3	8 × 6	3 × 5	6 × 8

Name _____

Practice **Fives** and **Doubles**.

5 × 3	2 × 7	2 × 4	3 × 5	5 × 3	8 × 2	9 × 2
2 × 2	3 × 5	2 × 6	5 × 3	4 × 2	3 × 5	3 × 2
2 × 5	2 × 9	3 × 5	6 × 2	5 × 3	7 × 2	5 × 3
3 × 5	2 × 3	2 × 8	5 × 3	5 × 2	3 × 5	2 × 2

Practice **Fives**, **Count 5,6,7,8**, and **1 Group**.

3 × 5	2 × 1	8 × 7	4 × 1	3 × 5	7 × 8	1 × 8
1 × 1	3 × 5	1 × 7	7 × 8	1 × 5	5 × 3	9 × 1
8 × 7	1 × 3	5 × 3	8 × 1	3 × 5	6 × 1	8 × 7
3 × 5	7 × 8	5 × 1	5 × 3	1 × 9	7 × 8	1 × 4

Name _____

Practice **Fives**, **4 Fingers**, and **Zero**.

3	4	3	5	3	4	0
$\times 5$	$\times 4$	$\times 4$	$\times 0$	$\times 5$	$\times 3$	$\times 8$

4	3	9	4	1	5	3
$\times 3$	$\times 5$	$\times 0$	$\times 4$	$\times 0$	$\times 3$	$\times 4$

3	0	5	4	3	4	3
$\times 5$	$\times 6$	$\times 3$	$\times 0$	$\times 4$	$\times 4$	$\times 5$

2	4	4	5	0	0	4
$\times 0$	$\times 3$	$\times 4$	$\times 3$	$\times 7$	$\times 3$	$\times 3$

Practice **Fives**, **Pretend to Add with 9**, and **I See 2 5s**.

$3 \times 5 =$ _____ $7 \times 9 =$ _____ $5 \times 3 =$ _____ $5 \times 5 =$ _____

$4 \times 9 =$ _____ $9 \times 9 =$ _____ $5 \times 5 =$ _____ $3 \times 5 =$ _____

$5 \times 3 =$ _____ $9 \times 4 =$ _____ $3 \times 5 =$ _____ $9 \times 7 =$ _____

$5 \times 5 =$ _____ $3 \times 5 =$ _____ $4 \times 9 =$ _____ $5 \times 3 =$ _____

$7 \times 9 =$ _____ $4 \times 9 =$ _____ $5 \times 3 =$ _____ $9 \times 9 =$ _____

$9 \times 4 =$ _____ $5 \times 3 =$ _____ $9 \times 7 =$ _____ $3 \times 5 =$ _____

Name _____

Practice **Fives** and **Count by 3s**.

3 $\times$ 5	3 $\times$ 3	3 $\times$ 6	6 $\times$ 3	3 $\times$ 5	5 $\times$ 3	3 $\times$ 3
3 $\times$ 6	5 $\times$ 3	6 $\times$ 3	3 $\times$ 5	3 $\times$ 3	3 $\times$ 6	5 $\times$ 3
3 $\times$ 3	3 $\times$ 5	3 $\times$ 3	3 $\times$ 6	5 $\times$ 3	6 $\times$ 3	3 $\times$ 5
5 $\times$ 3	3 $\times$ 6	3 $\times$ 5	3 $\times$ 3	6 $\times$ 3	5 $\times$ 3	6 $\times$ 3

Practice **Fives** and **Count by 3s** with addition and subtraction.

$3\times5=$ _____	$6+3=$ _____	$6\times3=$ _____	$5\times3=$ _____
$3+3=$ _____	$3\times6=$ _____	$3\times5=$ _____	$5-3=$ _____
$6\times3=$ _____	$3+5=$ _____	$3\times3=$ _____	$3\times6=$ _____
$6-3=$ _____	$3\times5=$ _____	$6-5=$ _____	$5\times0=$ _____
$5\times3=$ _____	$5+0=$ _____	$3\times6=$ _____	$5+3=$ _____
$3\times3=$ _____	$5\times3=$ _____	$3+6=$ _____	$6\times3=$ _____

Name _____

Cumulative Practice.

2 × 2	3 × 5	9 × 4	8 × 6	1 × 4	5 × 3	7 × 9
3 × 4	8 × 7	2 × 3	5 × 5	4 × 4	3 × 0	3 × 5
0 × 5	6 × 3	6 × 6	4 × 9	5 × 3	7 × 8	9 × 9
6 × 8	9 × 7	3 × 3	8 × 2	4 × 3	5 × 1	3 × 6
4 × 3	3 × 5	8 × 7	8 × 0	6 × 3	2 × 9	4 × 4
7 × 9	4 × 9	4 × 2	3 × 5	9 × 4	6 × 6	5 × 5
2 × 7	3 × 6	0 × 1	8 × 6	3 × 3	9 × 9	5 × 3
5 × 3	6 × 8	3 × 4	3 × 1	7 × 8	3 × 5	9 × 7

Name _____

Cumulative Practice.

8 × 6	1 × 8	5 × 3	4 × 9	3 × 5	6 × 2	9 × 9
1 × 1	6 × 3	0 × 2	4 × 3	7 × 9	6 × 8	6 × 6
3 × 3	5 × 5	8 × 7	5 × 3	2 × 8	9 × 4	3 × 5
9 × 7	8 × 1	3 × 4	7 × 8	8 × 6	5 × 3	6 × 0
6 × 6	5 × 3	9 × 4	9 × 7	3 × 4	1 × 2	2 × 5
9 × 2	6 × 1	5 × 5	9 × 9	9 × 0	3 × 5	7 × 8
3 × 6	4 × 4	6 × 8	5 × 3	8 × 7	4 × 9	4 × 3
3 × 5	2 × 4	6 × 3	7 × 9	3 × 5	0 × 6	3 × 6

Name _____

More **Pretend to Add with 9**

$$\begin{array}{r} 9 \\ \times\ 6 \\ \hline 54 \end{array}$$

Looks hard, so
<u>Pretend to Add with 9</u>

$$\begin{array}{r} 9 \\ +\ 6 \\ \hline \end{array}$$

to get the sound that starts **fif**teen

$5 + \underline{\ ?\ } = 9$

$5 + \underline{\ 4\ } = 9$

54

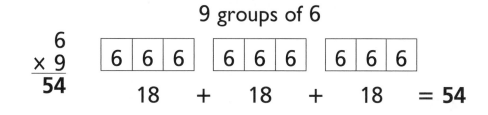

9 groups of 6

$$\begin{array}{r} 6 \\ \times\ 9 \\ \hline 54 \end{array}$$

| 6 | 6 | 6 | | 6 | 6 | 6 | | 6 | 6 | 6 |

18   +   18   +   18   = **54**

These are the same.

$$\begin{array}{r} 6 \\ \times\ 9 \\ \hline 54 \end{array} \qquad \begin{array}{r} 9 \\ \times\ 6 \\ \hline 54 \end{array}$$

Practice **Pretend to Add with 9**.

$$\begin{array}{r} 9 \\ \times\ 6 \\ \hline \end{array} \qquad \begin{array}{r} 6 \\ \times\ 9 \\ \hline \end{array} \qquad \begin{array}{r} 9 \\ \times\ 9 \\ \hline \end{array} \qquad \begin{array}{r} 9 \\ \times\ 7 \\ \hline \end{array} \qquad \begin{array}{r} 6 \\ \times\ 9 \\ \hline \end{array} \qquad \begin{array}{r} 9 \\ \times\ 4 \\ \hline \end{array} \qquad \begin{array}{r} 9 \\ \times\ 6 \\ \hline \end{array}$$

$$\begin{array}{r} 7 \\ \times\ 9 \\ \hline \end{array} \qquad \begin{array}{r} 9 \\ \times\ 9 \\ \hline \end{array} \qquad \begin{array}{r} 6 \\ \times\ 9 \\ \hline \end{array} \qquad \begin{array}{r} 4 \\ \times\ 9 \\ \hline \end{array} \qquad \begin{array}{r} 9 \\ \times\ 7 \\ \hline \end{array} \qquad \begin{array}{r} 9 \\ \times\ 6 \\ \hline \end{array} \qquad \begin{array}{r} 4 \\ \times\ 9 \\ \hline \end{array}$$

$$\begin{array}{r} 9 \\ \times\ 4 \\ \hline \end{array} \qquad \begin{array}{r} 9 \\ \times\ 6 \\ \hline \end{array} \qquad \begin{array}{r} 9 \\ \times\ 7 \\ \hline \end{array} \qquad \begin{array}{r} 6 \\ \times\ 9 \\ \hline \end{array} \qquad \begin{array}{r} 4 \\ \times\ 9 \\ \hline \end{array} \qquad \begin{array}{r} 9 \\ \times\ 9 \\ \hline \end{array} \qquad \begin{array}{r} 7 \\ \times\ 9 \\ \hline \end{array}$$

Name _____

Practice **Pretend to Add with 9** and **1 Group**.

6 × 9	9 × 1	9 × 4	6 × 9	1 × 4	9 × 6	9 × 9
1 × 7	9 × 6	9 × 7	1 × 3	7 × 9	4 × 9	9 × 6
7 × 9	9 × 9	6 × 9	9 × 4	2 × 1	6 × 1	4 × 9
4 × 9	1 × 8	5 × 1	9 × 7	9 × 6	9 × 7	6 × 9

Practice **Pretend to Add with 9** and **Rhymes**.

7 × 9	9 × 6	8 × 6	9 × 4	6 × 9	8 × 6	4 × 9
6 × 9	6 × 8	9 × 7	6 × 8	6 × 6	9 × 6	9 × 9
6 × 8	4 × 9	9 × 6	6 × 6	9 × 4	7 × 9	6 × 9
9 × 6	8 × 6	9 × 4	6 × 9	6 × 8	6 × 6	9 × 7

Name _____

Practice **Pretend to Add with 9** and **Fives**.

$$4 \times 9 \qquad 9 \times 6 \qquad 5 \times 3 \qquad 6 \times 9 \qquad 5 \times 3 \qquad 9 \times 7 \qquad 3 \times 5$$

$$9 \times 6 \qquad 5 \times 3 \qquad 9 \times 9 \qquad 9 \times 4 \qquad 6 \times 9 \qquad 3 \times 5 \qquad 7 \times 9$$

$$3 \times 5 \qquad 9 \times 7 \qquad 9 \times 6 \qquad 5 \times 3 \qquad 7 \times 9 \qquad 4 \times 9 \qquad 6 \times 9$$

$$7 \times 9 \qquad 6 \times 9 \qquad 5 \times 3 \qquad 9 \times 9 \qquad 9 \times 4 \qquad 9 \times 6 \qquad 9 \times 9$$

Practice **Pretend to Add with 9** and **4 Fingers**.

$$6 \times 9 \qquad 9 \times 4 \qquad 7 \times 9 \qquad 3 \times 4 \qquad 4 \times 4 \qquad 9 \times 6 \qquad 4 \times 3$$

$$4 \times 9 \qquad 9 \times 6 \qquad 3 \times 4 \qquad 6 \times 9 \qquad 4 \times 9 \qquad 9 \times 7 \qquad 6 \times 9$$

$$9 \times 9 \qquad 9 \times 7 \qquad 4 \times 4 \qquad 4 \times 3 \qquad 6 \times 9 \qquad 9 \times 4 \qquad 9 \times 7$$

$$9 \times 6 \qquad 4 \times 3 \qquad 4 \times 9 \qquad 7 \times 9 \qquad 9 \times 4 \qquad 3 \times 4 \qquad 9 \times 6$$

Name _____

Practice **Pretend to Add with 9**, **Count by 3s**, and **Count 5, 6, 7, 8**.

$9 \times 6 =$ _____ $7 \times 8 =$ _____ $9 \times 4 =$ _____ $3 \times 6 =$ _____

$7 \times 9 =$ _____ $3 \times 3 =$ _____ $6 \times 9 =$ _____ $8 \times 7 =$ _____

$6 \times 3 =$ _____ $4 \times 9 =$ _____ $8 \times 7 =$ _____ $9 \times 6 =$ _____

$7 \times 8 =$ _____ $9 \times 7 =$ _____ $6 \times 9 =$ _____ $9 \times 4 =$ _____

$3 \times 3 =$ _____ $9 \times 6 =$ _____ $6 \times 3 =$ _____ $7 \times 8 =$ _____

$6 \times 9 =$ _____ $3 \times 6 =$ _____ $4 \times 9 =$ _____ $7 \times 9 =$ _____

Cumulative Practice.

| $\begin{array}{r}9\\ \times 7\end{array}$ | $\begin{array}{r}4\\ \times 4\end{array}$ | $\begin{array}{r}3\\ \times 3\end{array}$ | $\begin{array}{r}6\\ \times 9\end{array}$ | $\begin{array}{r}0\\ \times 6\end{array}$ | $\begin{array}{r}9\\ \times 4\end{array}$ | $\begin{array}{r}5\\ \times 3\end{array}$ |

| $\begin{array}{r}1\\ \times 4\end{array}$ | $\begin{array}{r}8\\ \times 6\end{array}$ | $\begin{array}{r}2\\ \times 4\end{array}$ | $\begin{array}{r}6\\ \times 6\end{array}$ | $\begin{array}{r}3\\ \times 6\end{array}$ | $\begin{array}{r}9\\ \times 9\end{array}$ | $\begin{array}{r}9\\ \times 6\end{array}$ |

| $\begin{array}{r}7\\ \times 2\end{array}$ | $\begin{array}{r}3\\ \times 5\end{array}$ | $\begin{array}{r}7\\ \times 8\end{array}$ | $\begin{array}{r}3\\ \times 4\end{array}$ | $\begin{array}{r}9\\ \times 6\end{array}$ | $\begin{array}{r}8\\ \times 1\end{array}$ | $\begin{array}{r}6\\ \times 8\end{array}$ |

| $\begin{array}{r}4\\ \times 9\end{array}$ | $\begin{array}{r}6\\ \times 3\end{array}$ | $\begin{array}{r}5\\ \times 5\end{array}$ | $\begin{array}{r}6\\ \times 9\end{array}$ | $\begin{array}{r}7\\ \times 9\end{array}$ | $\begin{array}{r}8\\ \times 7\end{array}$ | $\begin{array}{r}4\\ \times 3\end{array}$ |

More **Pretend to Add with 9**

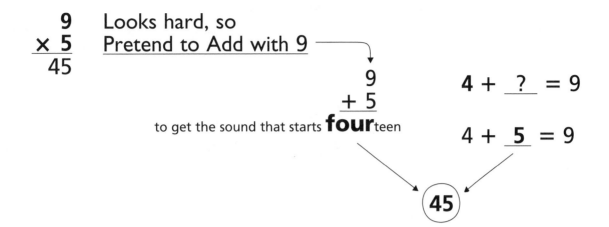

$$\begin{array}{r} 9 \\ \times\ 5 \\ \hline 45 \end{array}$$

Looks hard, so
<u>Pretend to Add with 9</u>

$$\begin{array}{r} 9 \\ +\ 5 \end{array}$$

to get the sound that starts **four**teen

$4 + \underline{\ ?\ } = 9$

$4 + \underline{\ 5\ } = 9$

(**45**)

9 groups of 5

$$\begin{array}{r} 5 \\ \times\ 9 \\ \hline 45 \end{array}$$

| 5 | 5 | 5 | | 5 | 5 | 5 | | 5 | 5 | 5 |

15 + 15 + 15 = **45**

These are the same.

$$\begin{array}{r} 5 \\ \times\ 9 \\ \hline 45 \end{array} \qquad \begin{array}{r} 9 \\ \times\ 5 \\ \hline 45 \end{array}$$

Practice **Pretend to Add with 9** and **Zero**.

$$\begin{array}{r} 5 \\ \times\ 9 \\ \hline \end{array} \quad \begin{array}{r} 9 \\ \times\ 7 \\ \hline \end{array} \quad \begin{array}{r} 9 \\ \times\ 5 \\ \hline \end{array} \quad \begin{array}{r} 0 \\ \times\ 9 \\ \hline \end{array} \quad \begin{array}{r} 6 \\ \times\ 9 \\ \hline \end{array} \quad \begin{array}{r} 5 \\ \times\ 9 \\ \hline \end{array} \quad \begin{array}{r} 9 \\ \times\ 4 \\ \hline \end{array}$$

$$\begin{array}{r} 9 \\ \times\ 6 \\ \hline \end{array} \quad \begin{array}{r} 9 \\ \times\ 5 \\ \hline \end{array} \quad \begin{array}{r} 6 \\ \times\ 0 \\ \hline \end{array} \quad \begin{array}{r} 9 \\ \times\ 9 \\ \hline \end{array} \quad \begin{array}{r} 0 \\ \times\ 7 \\ \hline \end{array} \quad \begin{array}{r} 6 \\ \times\ 9 \\ \hline \end{array} \quad \begin{array}{r} 5 \\ \times\ 0 \\ \hline \end{array}$$

$$\begin{array}{r} 4 \\ \times\ 9 \\ \hline \end{array} \quad \begin{array}{r} 0 \\ \times\ 6 \\ \hline \end{array} \quad \begin{array}{r} 7 \\ \times\ 9 \\ \hline \end{array} \quad \begin{array}{r} 9 \\ \times\ 5 \\ \hline \end{array} \quad \begin{array}{r} 9 \\ \times\ 6 \\ \hline \end{array} \quad \begin{array}{r} 4 \\ \times\ 0 \\ \hline \end{array} \quad \begin{array}{r} 5 \\ \times\ 9 \\ \hline \end{array}$$

Name _____

Practice **Pretend to Add with 9**, **1 Group**, and **Rhymes**.

$$\begin{array}{ccccccc}
7 & 9 & 8 & 9 & 5 & 1 & 8 \\
\times 9 & \times 5 & \times 1 & \times 6 & \times 9 & \times 6 & \times 6
\end{array}$$

$$\begin{array}{ccccccc}
6 & 9 & 9 & 9 & 6 & 9 & 5 \\
\times 6 & \times 1 & \times 4 & \times 5 & \times 8 & \times 9 & \times 9
\end{array}$$

$$\begin{array}{ccccccc}
1 & 8 & 9 & 6 & 9 & 5 & 3 \\
\times 7 & \times 6 & \times 5 & \times 6 & \times 7 & \times 9 & \times 1
\end{array}$$

$$\begin{array}{ccccccc}
9 & 4 & 6 & 1 & 5 & 1 & 6 \\
\times 5 & \times 9 & \times 8 & \times 1 & \times 9 & \times 5 & \times 9
\end{array}$$

Practice **Pretend to Add with 9** and **Count by 3s**.

6×9= _____	3×3= _____	9×5= _____	7×9= _____
9×5= _____	4×9= _____	9×9= _____	5×9= _____
6×3= _____	9×7= _____	9×6= _____	3×6= _____
9×4= _____	5×9= _____	6×3= _____	9×6= _____
9×9= _____	3×3= _____	5×9= _____	9×4= _____
7×9= _____	9×5= _____	3×6= _____	9×5= _____

Five Times Five Is Not Ten: Make Multiplication Easy

Name _____

Practice **Pretend to Add with 9**, **I See 2 5s**, and **4 Fingers**.

5 × 9	4 × 3	9 × 7	9 × 5	9 × 6	5 × 5	4 × 4

3 × 4	6 × 9	9 × 5	4 × 9	5 × 9	4 × 3	7 × 9

5 × 5	9 × 4	4 × 4	3 × 4	9 × 6	9 × 5	9 × 4

5 × 9	7 × 9	4 × 3	5 × 9	5 × 5	6 × 9	9 × 5

Practice **Pretend to Add with 9** and **Doubles**.

9×5= _____   2×8= _____   9×4= _____   6×9= _____

7×9= _____   5×9= _____   2×7= _____   5×2= _____

9×6= _____   9×2= _____   6×9= _____   9×5= _____

2×6= _____   9×9= _____   5×9= _____   7×9= _____

4×9= _____   3×2= _____   9×7= _____   9×6= _____

5×9= _____   2×4= _____   9×5= _____   9×4= _____

Five Times Five Is Not Ten: Make Multiplication Easy

Name _____

Practice **Pretend to Add with 9**, **Count 5,6,7,8**, and **Fives**.

9	8	5	5	9	9	3
× 4	× 7	× 9	× 3	× 6	× 5	× 5

6	9	5	7	7	9	5
× 9	× 5	× 3	× 9	× 8	× 4	× 9

5	9	9	8	5	3	6
× 3	× 7	× 6	× 7	× 9	× 5	× 9

9	3	4	3	7	7	5
× 5	× 5	× 9	× 5	× 9	× 8	× 3

Practice **Pretend to Add with 9** with addition.

9	9	9	6	9	4	9
× 9	+ 7	× 5	× 9	+ 9	+ 9	× 7

9	9	5	9	4	9	5
× 4	× 6	+ 9	+ 6	× 9	+ 5	× 9

6	9	9	9	9	4	6
+ 9	× 9	× 6	× 5	+ 7	× 9	× 9

5	9	7	9	5	7	9
× 9	+ 4	+ 9	+ 9	× 5	× 9	+ 5

See 2 4s

Cut the 8 groups of 3 in half.

$$\begin{array}{r} 3 \\ \times\ 8 \\ \hline 24 \end{array}$$ groups of

| 3 | 3 | 3 | 3 | 3 | 3 | 3 | 3 |

You know 4 × 3 = 12.

| 3 | 3 | 3 | 3 | | 3 | 3 | 3 | 3 |

12   +   12   = 24

These are the same.

$$\begin{array}{r} 3 \\ \times\ 8 \\ \hline 24 \end{array} \qquad \begin{array}{r} 8 \\ \times\ 3 \\ \hline 24 \end{array}$$

Another way to remember these facts:

Cut the eight in half. See **two fours**.

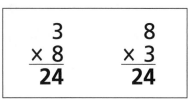

④ ④

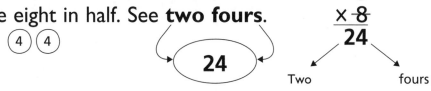

Two   fours

Remember this by saying, "I See 2 4s."

Practice **See 2 4s** and **Doubles**. (Circle) **See 2 4s**.

| $\begin{array}{r}3\\ \times 8\\ \hline\end{array}$ | $\begin{array}{r}2\\ \times 7\\ \hline\end{array}$ | $\begin{array}{r}8\\ \times 3\\ \hline\end{array}$ | $\begin{array}{r}9\\ \times 2\\ \hline\end{array}$ | $\begin{array}{r}3\\ \times 8\\ \hline\end{array}$ | $\begin{array}{r}3\\ \times 2\\ \hline\end{array}$ | $\begin{array}{r}8\\ \times 3\\ \hline\end{array}$ |

| $\begin{array}{r}4\\ \times 2\\ \hline\end{array}$ | $\begin{array}{r}3\\ \times 8\\ \hline\end{array}$ | $\begin{array}{r}2\\ \times 5\\ \hline\end{array}$ | $\begin{array}{r}2\\ \times 8\\ \hline\end{array}$ | $\begin{array}{r}2\\ \times 3\\ \hline\end{array}$ | $\begin{array}{r}8\\ \times 3\\ \hline\end{array}$ | $\begin{array}{r}6\\ \times 2\\ \hline\end{array}$ |

| $\begin{array}{r}8\\ \times 3\\ \hline\end{array}$ | $\begin{array}{r}3\\ \times 2\\ \hline\end{array}$ | $\begin{array}{r}3\\ \times 8\\ \hline\end{array}$ | $\begin{array}{r}8\\ \times 3\\ \hline\end{array}$ | $\begin{array}{r}8\\ \times 2\\ \hline\end{array}$ | $\begin{array}{r}2\\ \times 9\\ \hline\end{array}$ | $\begin{array}{r}3\\ \times 8\\ \hline\end{array}$ |

Name _____

Practice **See 2 4s**, **1 Group**, and **4 Fingers**.

8	8	3	3	1	4	8
× 3	× 1	× 4	× 8	× 4	× 3	× 3

3	8	1	4	4	3	3
× 4	× 3	× 3	× 3	× 4	× 8	× 4

4	4	3	8	1	3	3
× 1	× 4	× 8	× 3	× 8	× 4	× 8

8	1	4	4	3	3	4
× 3	× 1	× 3	× 4	× 8	× 1	× 3

Practice **See 2 4s** with addition and subtraction.

8×3= _____   3+8= _____   3×8= _____   8+8= _____

3−0= _____   3×8= _____   3−3= _____   8×3= _____

3×8= _____   3+0= _____   8×3= _____   8−1= _____

8+1= _____   3−1= _____   8+3= _____   0+8= _____

3+3= _____   8×3= _____   8−8= _____   3×8= _____

8×3= _____   8−0= _____   3×8= _____   1+3= _____

Name _____

Practice **See 2 4s** and **Pretend to Add with 9**.

3 × 8	7 × 9	5 × 9	8 × 3	9 × 6	3 × 8	9 × 4
9 × 9	8 × 3	3 × 8	9 × 7	8 × 3	4 × 9	7 × 9
8 × 3	9 × 5	9 × 4	9 × 6	5 × 9	6 × 9	3 × 8
6 × 9	4 × 9	9 × 9	3 × 8	9 × 7	8 × 3	9 × 5

Practice **See 2 4s**, **Count 5,6,7,8**, and **Count by 3s**.

8 × 3	8 × 7	3 × 8	3 × 3	6 × 3	3 × 6	7 × 8
3 × 6	3 × 8	6 × 3	8 × 7	8 × 3	7 × 8	3 × 3
7 × 8	6 × 3	8 × 7	3 × 8	3 × 3	6 × 3	8 × 3
3 × 8	7 × 8	8 × 3	3 × 6	8 × 7	3 × 8	3 × 6

Name _____

Practice **See 2 4s**, **Rhymes**, and **Zero**.

8 × 3	8 × 6	6 × 6	8 × 0	3 × 8	8 × 3	0 × 6
6 × 6	3 × 8	6 × 8	8 × 3	3 × 0	0 × 8	3 × 8
8 × 6	6 × 0	8 × 3	6 × 8	8 × 3	6 × 8	6 × 6
3 × 8	6 × 6	0 × 3	3 × 8	8 × 6	3 × 0	8 × 3

Practice **See 2 4s**, **Fives**, and **I See 2 5s**.

3 × 8	5 × 3	8 × 3	3 × 8	5 × 5	3 × 8	5 × 3
3 × 5	8 × 3	5 × 5	3 × 5	3 × 8	3 × 5	8 × 3
5 × 5	3 × 5	3 × 8	8 × 3	3 × 5	5 × 5	5 × 3
8 × 3	3 × 8	5 × 3	5 × 5	8 × 3	5 × 3	5 × 5

Five Times Five Is Not Ten: Make Multiplication Easy

Name _____

Cumulative Practice.

3 × 8	5 × 9	7 × 1	4 × 2	4 × 4	9 × 6	6 × 6
9 × 7	3 × 5	8 × 3	5 × 3	6 × 8	7 × 0	8 × 3
1 × 6	3 × 8	8 × 7	9 × 5	3 × 8	2 × 5	3 × 4
8 × 6	0 × 4	3 × 6	8 × 3	4 × 9	3 × 3	6 × 9
8 × 2	9 × 6	3 × 8	5 × 5	5 × 9	8 × 3	0 × 0
8 × 3	4 × 3	8 × 6	2 × 1	7 × 8	2 × 9	3 × 8
3 × 5	7 × 9	6 × 9	3 × 8	9 × 4	5 × 3	6 × 8
2 × 2	8 × 3	1 × 5	0 × 3	6 × 3	9 × 9	9 × 5

Name _____

Cumulative Practice.

4	8	5	6	2	9	3
× 4	× 3	× 3	× 6	× 8	× 5	× 8

5	9	9	1	8	6	2
× 0	× 7	× 6	× 9	× 3	× 3	× 4

3	5	4	8	0	6	9
× 8	× 5	× 9	× 7	× 9	× 9	× 9

9	2	8	3	6	3	7
× 2	× 1	× 3	× 4	× 8	× 3	× 9

Practice this way.

2×2= _____   8×7= _____   3×2= _____   4×9= _____

3×8= _____   9×5= _____   7×9= _____   3×1= _____

5×3= _____   1×4= _____   6×3= _____   8×3= _____

5×9= _____   3×4= _____   4×4= _____   2×6= _____

6×8= _____   1×1= _____   0×2= _____   7×8= _____

2×5= _____   8×3= _____   4×9= _____   9×6= _____

Name _____

More 4 Fingers

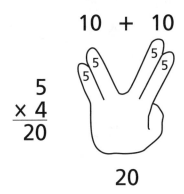

10 + 10

5
× 4
20

20

4 groups of 5

⊙ 10 ⊙ + ⊙ 10 ⊙

20

Draw 5 groups of 4.

These are the same.

5	4
× **4**	× 5
20	20

Practice **4 Fingers** and **See 2 4s**.

5	4	4	8	5	3	3
× 4	× 4	× 5	× 3	× 4	× 8	× 4

4	5	4	4	8	3	4
× 3	× 4	× 4	× 5	× 3	× 4	× 5

4	8	4	5	4	3	4
× 5	× 3	× 3	× 4	× 4	× 8	× 3

8	4	3	4	3	5	3
× 3	× 5	× 8	× 4	× 4	× 4	× 8

Name _____

Practice **4 Fingers** and **Count 5, 6, 7, 8**.

5 × 4	4 × 3	8 × 7	4 × 5	4 × 4	3 × 4	4 × 5
7 × 8	4 × 4	5 × 4	7 × 8	4 × 3	4 × 5	8 × 7
4 × 5	8 × 7	4 × 4	5 × 4	7 × 8	5 × 4	4 × 4
4 × 3	4 × 5	7 × 8	3 × 4	5 × 4	8 × 7	4 × 5

Practice **4 Fingers** and **Pretend to Add with 9**.

4 × 3	7 × 9	4 × 5	4 × 4	9 × 6	5 × 4	9 × 5
4 × 9	4 × 5	4 × 3	9 × 7	5 × 4	6 × 9	4 × 4
5 × 4	3 × 4	9 × 5	4 × 5	3 × 4	9 × 9	5 × 4
5 × 9	4 × 4	3 × 4	6 × 9	9 × 4	4 × 5	3 × 4

Name _____

Practice **4 Fingers**, **Fives**, and **I See 2 5s**.

4 × 5	5 × 3	4 × 4	5 × 4	5 × 5	3 × 4	5 × 3
3 × 5	5 × 4	4 × 3	5 × 5	4 × 5	5 × 3	5 × 4
5 × 5	4 × 4	4 × 5	4 × 3	3 × 5	5 × 5	3 × 4
5 × 4	5 × 3	3 × 4	4 × 5	4 × 3	3 × 5	4 × 4

Practice **4 Fingers** and **Rhymes**.

4×5= _____	6×8= _____	4×4= _____	6×6= _____
3×4= _____	4×5= _____	8×6= _____	4×3= _____
6×6= _____	4×3= _____	5×4= _____	4×5= _____
8×6= _____	5×4= _____	3×4= _____	6×8= _____
5×4= _____	4×4= _____	4×5= _____	3×4= _____
6×8= _____	6×6= _____	4×3= _____	5×4= _____

Name _____

Practice **4 Fingers**, **Count by 3s**, and **Doubles**.

4 × 5	8 × 2	3 × 6	4 × 4	2 × 7	4 × 3	5 × 4
3 × 3	3 × 4	9 × 2	5 × 4	6 × 3	4 × 5	5 × 2
3 × 6	2 × 3	3 × 4	6 × 2	3 × 3	2 × 2	6 × 3
4 × 3	5 × 4	6 × 3	4 × 4	2 × 4	3 × 6	4 × 5

Practice **4 Fingers** and **Zero** with addition and subtraction.

4 × 4	0 + 4	0 × 5	4 + 4	4 × 0	4 × 5	5 − 4
3 × 0	4 × 5	4 + 3	3 × 4	4 + 5	0 × 4	5 × 4
5 − 5	4 × 3	3 − 0	5 × 4	1 + 4	4 × 5	5 × 0
3 × 4	5 + 1	5 × 4	3 × 0	5 + 4	4 × 3	4 × 4

Five Times Five Is Not Ten: Make Multiplication Easy

More 4 Fingers

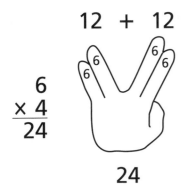

12 + 12

6
× 4
24

24

4 groups of 6

⊡⊡ ⊡⊡

⑫   +   ⑫

24

Draw 6 groups of 4.

These are the same.

6	**4**
× **4**	× **6**
24	24

Practice **4 Fingers** and **1 Group**. ⟨Circle⟩ **4 Fingers**.

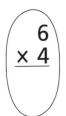

6	4	4	3	6	5	4
× 4	× 4	× 6	× 1	× 4	× 4	× 3

1	4	8	4	1	6	1
× 6	× 6	× 1	× 5	× 2	× 4	× 4

3	5	6	1	3	7	4
× 4	× 4	× 4	× 5	× 4	× 1	× 4

4	9	4	6	1	4	4
× 6	× 1	× 5	× 4	× 1	× 3	× 6

Name _____

Practice **4 Fingers** and **Doubles**.

4	3	5	6	2	6	5
× 6	× 4	× 2	× 4	× 4	× 4	× 4

2	4	6	7	4	4	4
× 8	× 5	× 4	× 2	× 4	× 3	× 6

4	2	4	5	4	2	6
× 2	× 3	× 4	× 4	× 6	× 9	× 2

4	6	2	4	3	4	8
× 5	× 4	× 2	× 3	× 4	× 6	× 2

Practice **4 Fingers** and **Fives**.

$4×3=$ _____ $6×4=$ _____ $3×5=$ _____ $4×6=$ _____

$5×3=$ _____ $4×5=$ _____ $4×4=$ _____ $4×5=$ _____

$6×4=$ _____ $4×6=$ _____ $5×4=$ _____ $3×5=$ _____

$4×6=$ _____ $5×4=$ _____ $5×3=$ _____ $3×4=$ _____

$4×4=$ _____ $5×3=$ _____ $4×5=$ _____ $6×4=$ _____

$3×4=$ _____ $6×4=$ _____ $3×5=$ _____ $4×3=$ _____

Name _____

Practice **4 Fingers** and **Rhymes**.

4 × 4	6 × 6	4 × 6	4 × 5	3 × 4	8 × 6	6 × 4
6 × 8	6 × 4	5 × 4	6 × 6	4 × 5	4 × 6	6 × 8
4 × 6	4 × 4	8 × 6	4 × 3	6 × 4	6 × 6	3 × 4
6 × 6	8 × 6	4 × 6	5 × 4	6 × 8	4 × 3	6 × 4

Practice **4 Fingers**, **Zero**, and **I See 2 5s**.

6 × 4	5 × 5	1 × 0	3 × 4	5 × 5	5 × 4	4 × 6
0 × 9	4 × 3	4 × 6	4 × 5	3 × 4	4 × 0	4 × 5
4 × 4	4 × 6	7 × 0	0 × 6	6 × 4	4 × 4	0 × 2
5 × 4	0 × 3	5 × 5	6 × 4	5 × 0	4 × 5	3 × 4

Name _____

Practice **4 Fingers**, **See 2 4s**, and **Count 5,6,7,8**.

4 × 3	3 × 8	8 × 7	4 × 4	3 × 4	7 × 8	4 × 6
8 × 3	6 × 4	5 × 4	7 × 8	4 × 5	4 × 6	3 × 8
6 × 4	8 × 7	4 × 4	4 × 3	6 × 4	8 × 3	3 × 4
7 × 8	5 × 4	4 × 6	3 × 8	8 × 7	4 × 5	8 × 3

Practice **4 Fingers** and **Pretend to Add with 9**.

4 × 5	9 × 5	4 × 6	4 × 3	6 × 4	4 × 4	9 × 9
7 × 9	6 × 4	5 × 4	9 × 5	6 × 9	4 × 6	3 × 4
9 × 4	3 × 4	9 × 6	7 × 9	4 × 9	9 × 7	4 × 6
4 × 4	5 × 9	6 × 4	6 × 9	4 × 5	4 × 9	9 × 6

More 4 Fingers

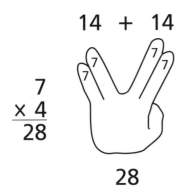

14 + 14

$$\begin{array}{r} 7 \\ \times\ 4 \\ \hline 28 \end{array}$$

28

4 groups of 7

14 + 14

28

These are the same.

Draw 7 groups of 4.

$$\begin{array}{r} 7 \\ \times\ \mathbf{4} \\ \hline 28 \end{array} \qquad \begin{array}{r} \mathbf{4} \\ \times\ 7 \\ \hline 28 \end{array}$$

Practice **4 Fingers**, **Count 5,6,7,8**, and **Zero**. (Circle) **4 Fingers**.

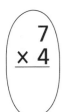

| $\begin{array}{r}7\\ \times\,4\\ \hline\end{array}$ | $\begin{array}{r}7\\ \times\,0\\ \hline\end{array}$ | $\begin{array}{r}6\\ \times\,4\\ \hline\end{array}$ | $\begin{array}{r}8\\ \times\,7\\ \hline\end{array}$ | $\begin{array}{r}0\\ \times\,8\\ \hline\end{array}$ | $\begin{array}{r}4\\ \times\,7\\ \hline\end{array}$ | $\begin{array}{r}4\\ \times\,4\\ \hline\end{array}$ |

| $\begin{array}{r}7\\ \times\,8\\ \hline\end{array}$ | $\begin{array}{r}4\\ \times\,7\\ \hline\end{array}$ | $\begin{array}{r}5\\ \times\,4\\ \hline\end{array}$ | $\begin{array}{r}7\\ \times\,4\\ \hline\end{array}$ | $\begin{array}{r}4\\ \times\,3\\ \hline\end{array}$ | $\begin{array}{r}0\\ \times\,4\\ \hline\end{array}$ | $\begin{array}{r}8\\ \times\,7\\ \hline\end{array}$ |

| $\begin{array}{r}4\\ \times\,6\\ \hline\end{array}$ | $\begin{array}{r}8\\ \times\,7\\ \hline\end{array}$ | $\begin{array}{r}7\\ \times\,4\\ \hline\end{array}$ | $\begin{array}{r}0\\ \times\,7\\ \hline\end{array}$ | $\begin{array}{r}7\\ \times\,8\\ \hline\end{array}$ | $\begin{array}{r}4\\ \times\,5\\ \hline\end{array}$ | $\begin{array}{r}4\\ \times\,7\\ \hline\end{array}$ |

| $\begin{array}{r}4\\ \times\,0\\ \hline\end{array}$ | $\begin{array}{r}4\\ \times\,7\\ \hline\end{array}$ | $\begin{array}{r}7\\ \times\,8\\ \hline\end{array}$ | $\begin{array}{r}6\\ \times\,4\\ \hline\end{array}$ | $\begin{array}{r}7\\ \times\,4\\ \hline\end{array}$ | $\begin{array}{r}8\\ \times\,0\\ \hline\end{array}$ | $\begin{array}{r}3\\ \times\,4\\ \hline\end{array}$ |

Name _____

Practice **4 Fingers** with addition and subtraction.

7 × 4	7 + 7	4 × 7	4 × 3	7 − 0	4 × 5	4 × 7
4 + 4	4 × 6	4 × 4	7 × 4	5 × 4	4 + 3	7 − 1
5 × 4	4 × 7	4 − 4	6 × 4	4 × 7	3 × 4	5 + 4
4 × 6	7 − 7	7 × 4	4 × 4	6 × 4	7 × 4	4 × 3

Practice **4 Fingers**, **I See 2 5s**, and **1 Group**.

4 × 6	7 × 4	4 × 1	3 × 4	4 × 7	5 × 5	4 × 5
4 × 7	1 × 6	3 × 4	5 × 5	4 × 6	7 × 1	7 × 4
4 × 4	5 × 5	7 × 4	1 × 7	4 × 3	4 × 7	1 × 4
1 × 5	5 × 4	6 × 1	4 × 7	4 × 5	6 × 4	5 × 5

Name _____

Practice **4 Fingers**, **Pretend to Add with 9**, and **See 2 4s**.

3 × 4	9 × 5	9 × 4	6 × 4	7 × 4	3 × 8	4 × 7
7 × 9	8 × 3	4 × 7	6 × 9	4 × 5	5 × 9	3 × 8
7 × 4	9 × 6	3 × 8	7 × 4	8 × 3	4 × 4	4 × 6
9 × 9	4 × 9	5 × 4	3 × 4	4 × 7	9 × 7	8 × 3

Practice **4 Fingers**, **Rhymes**, and **Fives**.

4 × 7	8 × 6	6 × 4	6 × 8	5 × 4	7 × 4	5 × 3
6 × 6	3 × 5	3 × 4	7 × 4	6 × 8	4 × 4	4 × 7
5 × 3	4 × 7	8 × 6	4 × 3	3 × 5	4 × 6	6 × 6
7 × 4	6 × 8	3 × 5	6 × 6	4 × 7	4 × 5	8 × 6

Five Times Five Is Not Ten: Make Multiplication Easy **91**

Name _____

Cumulative Practice.

$$\begin{array}{r} 5 \\ \times\ 4 \\ \hline \end{array} \qquad \begin{array}{r} 9 \\ \times\ 2 \\ \hline \end{array} \qquad \begin{array}{r} 4 \\ \times\ 7 \\ \hline \end{array} \qquad \begin{array}{r} 5 \\ \times\ 3 \\ \hline \end{array} \qquad \begin{array}{r} 7 \\ \times\ 9 \\ \hline \end{array} \qquad \begin{array}{r} 6 \\ \times\ 6 \\ \hline \end{array} \qquad \begin{array}{r} 3 \\ \times\ 4 \\ \hline \end{array}$$

$$\begin{array}{r} 2 \\ \times\ 5 \\ \hline \end{array} \qquad \begin{array}{r} 6 \\ \times\ 3 \\ \hline \end{array} \qquad \begin{array}{r} 5 \\ \times\ 0 \\ \hline \end{array} \qquad \begin{array}{r} 7 \\ \times\ 4 \\ \hline \end{array} \qquad \begin{array}{r} 8 \\ \times\ 6 \\ \hline \end{array} \qquad \begin{array}{r} 1 \\ \times\ 3 \\ \hline \end{array} \qquad \begin{array}{r} 8 \\ \times\ 3 \\ \hline \end{array}$$

$$\begin{array}{r} 9 \\ \times\ 5 \\ \hline \end{array} \qquad \begin{array}{r} 6 \\ \times\ 8 \\ \hline \end{array} \qquad \begin{array}{r} 3 \\ \times\ 3 \\ \hline \end{array} \qquad \begin{array}{r} 8 \\ \times\ 7 \\ \hline \end{array} \qquad \begin{array}{r} 6 \\ \times\ 4 \\ \hline \end{array} \qquad \begin{array}{r} 9 \\ \times\ 6 \\ \hline \end{array} \qquad \begin{array}{r} 4 \\ \times\ 4 \\ \hline \end{array}$$

$$\begin{array}{r} 3 \\ \times\ 8 \\ \hline \end{array} \qquad \begin{array}{r} 4 \\ \times\ 7 \\ \hline \end{array} \qquad \begin{array}{r} 3 \\ \times\ 5 \\ \hline \end{array} \qquad \begin{array}{r} 6 \\ \times\ 1 \\ \hline \end{array} \qquad \begin{array}{r} 4 \\ \times\ 5 \\ \hline \end{array} \qquad \begin{array}{r} 7 \\ \times\ 2 \\ \hline \end{array} \qquad \begin{array}{r} 9 \\ \times\ 4 \\ \hline \end{array}$$

Practice this way.

$6 \times 3 =$ _____ $8 \times 7 =$ _____ $6 \times 4 =$ _____ $4 \times 0 =$ _____

$8 \times 2 =$ _____ $5 \times 5 =$ _____ $9 \times 4 =$ _____ $8 \times 3 =$ _____

$3 \times 4 =$ _____ $4 \times 7 =$ _____ $2 \times 1 =$ _____ $5 \times 3 =$ _____

$3 \times 8 =$ _____ $9 \times 9 =$ _____ $7 \times 8 =$ _____ $6 \times 6 =$ _____

$7 \times 4 =$ _____ $8 \times 6 =$ _____ $2 \times 6 =$ _____ $7 \times 9 =$ _____

$9 \times 5 =$ _____ $3 \times 6 =$ _____ $4 \times 7 =$ _____ $6 \times 9 =$ _____

Pretend to Add

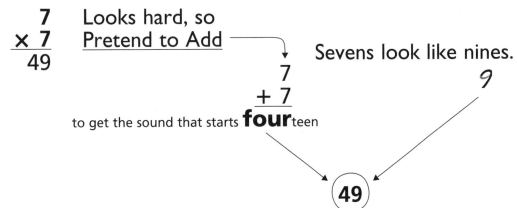

$$\begin{array}{r} 7 \\ \times\ 7 \\ \hline 49 \end{array}$$

Looks hard, so
<u>Pretend to Add</u>

Sevens look like nines.

$$\begin{array}{r} 7 \\ +\ 7 \\ \hline \end{array}$$

to get the sound that starts **four**teen

⑨

(49)

Draw 7 groups of 7.

Practice **Pretend to Add** with addition and subtraction.

7×7= _____	7−1= _____	7×7= _____	7+7= _____
14−7= _____	0×7= _____	1+7= _____	7×7= _____
7+0= _____	7×7= _____	7−0= _____	0+7= _____
7×7= _____	7−7= _____	7×7= _____	7+1= _____

Practice **Pretend to Add** and **Count 5,6,7,8**.

7 ×7	8 ×7	7 ×7	7 ×8	8 ×7	7 ×7	7 ×8

8 ×7	7 ×7	7 ×8	7 ×7	7 ×8	8 ×7	7 ×7

Name _____

Practice **Pretend to Add** and **4 Fingers**.

7 × 7	6 × 4	4 × 7	7 × 7	3 × 4	7 × 7	4 × 5
7 × 4	4 × 4	7 × 7	5 × 4	7 × 7	7 × 4	4 × 3
4 × 5	7 × 7	6 × 4	7 × 7	4 × 7	3 × 4	7 × 7
4 × 6	7 × 4	7 × 7	4 × 3	5 × 4	7 × 7	4 × 6

Practice **Pretend to Add** and **Pretend to Add with 9**.

7 × 7	9 × 6	4 × 9	7 × 7	5 × 9	9 × 4	7 × 7
6 × 9	9 × 5	7 × 7	9 × 9	6 × 9	7 × 7	7 × 9
9 × 9	7 × 7	9 × 7	4 × 9	7 × 7	5 × 9	9 × 4
7 × 7	7 × 9	9 × 6	9 × 7	9 × 5	7 × 7	9 × 9

Name _____

Practice **Pretend to Add**, **Count by 3s**, and **1 Group**.

$$7 \times 7 \qquad 2 \times 1 \qquad 3 \times 6 \qquad 3 \times 3 \qquad 1 \times 8 \qquad 7 \times 7 \qquad 1 \times 5$$

$$6 \times 3 \qquad 1 \times 7 \qquad 7 \times 7 \qquad 3 \times 6 \qquad 3 \times 1 \qquad 3 \times 3 \qquad 7 \times 7$$

$$1 \times 3 \qquad 7 \times 7 \qquad 3 \times 3 \qquad 4 \times 1 \qquad 7 \times 7 \qquad 6 \times 3 \qquad 9 \times 1$$

$$3 \times 3 \qquad 3 \times 6 \qquad 1 \times 6 \qquad 7 \times 7 \qquad 6 \times 3 \qquad 7 \times 1 \qquad 3 \times 3$$

Practice **Pretend to Add**, **Rhymes**, and **Doubles**.

$7 \times 7 =$ _____ $6 \times 6 =$ _____ $2 \times 4 =$ _____ $6 \times 8 =$ _____

$5 \times 2 =$ _____ $2 \times 7 =$ _____ $8 \times 6 =$ _____ $7 \times 7 =$ _____

$2 \times 8 =$ _____ $8 \times 6 =$ _____ $7 \times 7 =$ _____ $9 \times 2 =$ _____

$6 \times 6 =$ _____ $7 \times 7 =$ _____ $3 \times 2 =$ _____ $6 \times 8 =$ _____

$2 \times 2 =$ _____ $6 \times 2 =$ _____ $6 \times 8 =$ _____ $7 \times 7 =$ _____

$7 \times 2 =$ _____ $6 \times 6 =$ _____ $7 \times 7 =$ _____ $8 \times 6 =$ _____

Name _____

Practice **Pretend to Add**, **See 2 4s**, and **Fives**.

7	8	3	7	3	8	5
× 7	× 3	× 8	× 7	× 5	× 3	× 3

3	7	5	8	7	5	7
× 8	× 7	× 3	× 3	× 7	× 3	× 7

8	5	7	3	3	7	3
× 3	× 3	× 7	× 5	× 8	× 7	× 5

5	7	3	3	3	8	7
× 3	× 7	× 5	× 8	× 5	× 3	× 7

Cumulative Practice.

$3 \times 3 =$ _____ $7 \times 7 =$ _____ $9 \times 5 =$ _____ $4 \times 6 =$ _____

$3 \times 8 =$ _____ $5 \times 5 =$ _____ $6 \times 6 =$ _____ $4 \times 9 =$ _____

$9 \times 1 =$ _____ $3 \times 4 =$ _____ $0 \times 8 =$ _____ $6 \times 8 =$ _____

$7 \times 7 =$ _____ $9 \times 7 =$ _____ $3 \times 6 =$ _____ $1 \times 8 =$ _____

$5 \times 4 =$ _____ $2 \times 6 =$ _____ $6 \times 9 =$ _____ $7 \times 4 =$ _____

$8 \times 7 =$ _____ $4 \times 7 =$ _____ $7 \times 7 =$ _____ $5 \times 3 =$ _____

More **Pretend to Add**

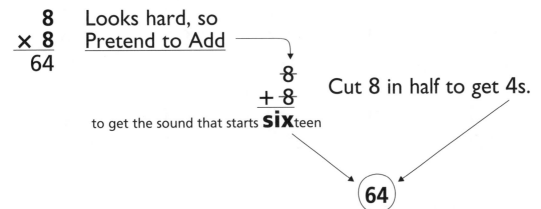

$$\begin{array}{r} 8 \\ \times\, 8 \\ \hline 64 \end{array}$$ Looks hard, so
Pretend to Add

$$\begin{array}{r} 8 \\ +\, 8 \end{array}$$ Cut 8 in half to get 4s.

to get the sound that starts **six**teen

64

Draw 8 groups of 8.

Practice **Pretend to Add** with addition and subtraction.

8×8= _____	8−1= _____	8×8= _____	7×7= _____
7−7= _____	8×8= _____	8+1= _____	7−1= _____
7×7= _____	8−8= _____	7×7= _____	8×8= _____
8+8= _____	7×7= _____	8×8= _____	7+7= _____

Practice **Pretend to Add** and **See 2 4s**.

8 × 8	7 × 7	8 × 8	3 × 8	7 × 7	8 × 3	7 × 7

3 × 8	8 × 8	8 × 3	8 × 8	3 × 8	7 × 7	8 × 8

Name _____

Practice **Pretend to Add**, **I See 2 5s**, and **Pretend to Add with 9**.

8	9	8	7	9	8	7
× 8	× 4	× 8	× 7	× 5	× 8	× 9

7	5	9	9	8	4	7
× 7	× 5	× 6	× 9	× 8	× 9	× 7

5	7	8	9	5	5	8
× 9	× 7	× 8	× 7	× 5	× 9	× 8

9	7	5	8	6	8	9
× 6	× 9	× 5	× 8	× 9	× 8	× 4

Practice **Pretend to Add**, **Doubles**, and **Count 5,6,7,8**.

7	3	8	7	8	5	8
× 7	× 2	× 8	× 2	× 7	× 2	× 8

2	8	7	7	2	8	7
× 8	× 8	× 7	× 8	× 9	× 8	× 8

8	7	2	8	8	7	6
× 8	× 7	× 4	× 8	× 7	× 7	× 2

2	7	8	8	2	8	8
× 2	× 8	× 8	× 7	× 7	× 8	× 2

Name _____

Practice **Pretend to Add**, **Zero**, and **Count by 3s**.

7 × 7	0 × 8	3 × 6	8 × 8	7 × 7	6 × 3	6 × 0
8 × 8	6 × 3	8 × 8	3 × 3	3 × 6	0 × 7	8 × 8
3 × 0	8 × 8	0 × 6	6 × 3	8 × 0	8 × 8	7 × 7
6 × 3	1 × 0	7 × 7	7 × 0	8 × 8	3 × 3	0 × 3

Practice **Pretend to Add**, **Rhymes**, and **4 Fingers**.

8×8= _____	6×8= _____	4×7= _____	8×8= _____
4×5= _____	6×6= _____	8×6= _____	4×6= _____
7×7= _____	7×4= _____	4×4= _____	7×7= _____
8×6= _____	7×7= _____	8×8= _____	4×3= _____
6×6= _____	6×4= _____	6×6= _____	6×8= _____
3×4= _____	8×8= _____	7×7= _____	5×4= _____

Name _____

Cumulative Practice.

8 × 2	9 × 7	3 × 4	8 × 8	4 × 7	3 × 6	2 × 0
7 × 4	3 × 5	7 × 7	4 × 9	8 × 6	4 × 4	9 × 5
8 × 8	1 × 1	4 × 5	7 × 8	4 × 6	3 × 8	2 × 6
9 × 9	9 × 6	8 × 8	8 × 3	1 × 6	0 × 9	8 × 8
7 × 7	6 × 8	5 × 3	8 × 8	5 × 9	4 × 2	8 × 7
6 × 4	2 × 3	6 × 6	0 × 2	9 × 1	4 × 7	8 × 8
7 × 9	3 × 3	7 × 7	4 × 3	5 × 2	5 × 5	5 × 4
7 × 2	8 × 8	9 × 4	7 × 4	6 × 9	2 × 9	6 × 3

More Fives

Multiply with 5s and **even** numbers.

(You know **4 Fingers**: 4×5 and 5×4.)

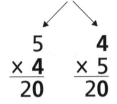

$$\begin{array}{r} 5 \\ \times\,4 \\ \hline 20 \end{array} \quad \begin{array}{r} \mathbf{4} \\ \times\,\mathbf{5} \\ \hline 20 \end{array}$$

Learn

$$\begin{array}{r} 5 \\ \times\,\mathbf{6} \\ \hline 30 \end{array} \quad \begin{array}{r} \mathbf{6} \\ \times\,5 \\ \hline 30 \end{array}$$

$$\begin{array}{r} 5 \\ \times\,\mathbf{8} \\ \hline 40 \end{array} \quad \begin{array}{r} \mathbf{8} \\ \times\,5 \\ \hline 40 \end{array}$$

Cut the **even** number in half, and these answers all end with a **zero**.

Cut **4** in half.
Get **2**
$$\begin{array}{r} \mathbf{4} \\ \times\,5 \\ \hline 2\underline{0} \end{array}$$

Cut **6** in half.
Get **3**
$$\begin{array}{r} \mathbf{6} \\ \times\,5 \\ \hline 3\underline{0} \end{array}$$

Cut **8** in half.
Get **4**
$$\begin{array}{r} \mathbf{8} \\ \times\,5 \\ \hline 4\underline{0} \end{array}$$

Practice **Fives**. Cut ~~4~~, ~~6~~, and ~~8~~ in half.

$$\begin{array}{r} \cancel{6} \\ \times\,5 \\ \hline \end{array} \quad \begin{array}{r} \cancel{8} \\ \times\,5 \\ \hline \end{array} \quad \begin{array}{r} \cancel{4} \\ \times\,5 \\ \hline \end{array} \quad \begin{array}{r} 8 \\ \times\,5 \\ \hline \end{array} \quad \begin{array}{r} 6 \\ \times\,5 \\ \hline \end{array} \quad \begin{array}{r} 5 \\ \times\,3 \\ \hline \end{array} \quad \begin{array}{r} 4 \\ \times\,5 \\ \hline \end{array}$$

$$\begin{array}{r} 5 \\ \times\,8 \\ \hline \end{array} \quad \begin{array}{r} 5 \\ \times\,4 \\ \hline \end{array} \quad \begin{array}{r} 3 \\ \times\,5 \\ \hline \end{array} \quad \begin{array}{r} 5 \\ \times\,6 \\ \hline \end{array} \quad \begin{array}{r} 5 \\ \times\,8 \\ \hline \end{array} \quad \begin{array}{r} 4 \\ \times\,5 \\ \hline \end{array} \quad \begin{array}{r} 5 \\ \times\,6 \\ \hline \end{array}$$

$$\begin{array}{r} 5 \\ \times\,3 \\ \hline \end{array} \quad \begin{array}{r} 6 \\ \times\,5 \\ \hline \end{array} \quad \begin{array}{r} 5 \\ \times\,4 \\ \hline \end{array} \quad \begin{array}{r} 5 \\ \times\,8 \\ \hline \end{array} \quad \begin{array}{r} 5 \\ \times\,6 \\ \hline \end{array} \quad \begin{array}{r} 3 \\ \times\,5 \\ \hline \end{array} \quad \begin{array}{r} 8 \\ \times\,5 \\ \hline \end{array}$$

$$\begin{array}{r} 8 \\ \times\,5 \\ \hline \end{array} \quad \begin{array}{r} 5 \\ \times\,4 \\ \hline \end{array} \quad \begin{array}{r} 5 \\ \times\,6 \\ \hline \end{array} \quad \begin{array}{r} 3 \\ \times\,5 \\ \hline \end{array} \quad \begin{array}{r} 5 \\ \times\,8 \\ \hline \end{array} \quad \begin{array}{r} 6 \\ \times\,5 \\ \hline \end{array} \quad \begin{array}{r} 5 \\ \times\,3 \\ \hline \end{array}$$

Name _____

Practice **Fives** and **I See 2 5s**.

5 × 6	8 × 5	5 × 4	6 × 5	5 × 5	8 × 5	5 × 3
5 × 5	6 × 5	3 × 5	5 × 8	8 × 5	4 × 5	5 × 6
5 × 8	5 × 3	5 × 5	3 × 5	5 × 4	6 × 5	5 × 5
6 × 5	4 × 5	5 × 6	5 × 8	3 × 5	5 × 5	8 × 5

Practice **Fives** and **Zero**.

5 × 8	5 × 4	8 × 0	5 × 6	0 × 5	5 × 3	0 × 4
0 × 6	6 × 5	5 × 8	2 × 0	8 × 5	6 × 5	5 × 4
5 × 6	3 × 5	5 × 0	5 × 8	6 × 0	4 × 5	3 × 5
4 × 5	8 × 5	5 × 3	6 × 5	8 × 5	0 × 8	5 × 6

Five Times Five Is Not Ten: Make Multiplication Easy

Name _____

Practice **Fives** and **Pretend to Add**. (Circle) **Fives**.

8	8	5	4	3	7	5
× 5	× 8	× 6	× 5	× 5	× 7	× 8

4	6	7	8	8	5	5
× 5	× 5	× 7	× 5	× 8	× 4	× 3

5	5	8	6	7	5	8
× 6	× 3	× 8	× 5	× 7	× 8	× 8

7	5	5	3	8	6	5
× 7	× 8	× 4	× 5	× 5	× 5	× 6

Practice **Fives** and **Doubles**.

6×5= _____   5×8= _____   3×5= _____   8×2= _____

2×2= _____   4×5= _____   2×6= _____   5×6= _____

8×5= _____   2×9= _____   8×2= _____   2×7= _____

3×5= _____   6×5= _____   2×2= _____   4×2= _____

5×2= _____   8×5= _____   5×4= _____   9×2= _____

5×6= _____   2×3= _____   5×8= _____   5×3= _____

Five Times Five Is Not Ten: Make Multiplication Easy

Name _____

Practice **Fives** and **See 2 4s**.

5 × 4	8 × 5	5 × 6	8 × 3	6 × 5	5 × 3	3 × 8
5 × 3	8 × 3	8 × 5	3 × 5	3 × 8	4 × 5	5 × 6
3 × 8	8 × 5	6 × 5	5 × 8	5 × 4	6 × 5	5 × 8
5 × 6	8 × 3	3 × 8	4 × 5	5 × 8	8 × 3	3 × 5

Practice **Fives** and **4 Fingers**.

8 × 5	5 × 6	4 × 4	3 × 4	5 × 8	7 × 4	6 × 4
5 × 3	4 × 5	5 × 8	5 × 4	6 × 5	4 × 6	4 × 7
5 × 6	4 × 3	3 × 5	4 × 7	3 × 4	8 × 5	4 × 5
4 × 4	7 × 4	4 × 6	5 × 8	6 × 4	4 × 3	6 × 5

Name _____

REVIEW

Practice **Fives**, **I See 2 5s**, and **Rhymes**.

5	5	8	8	5	6	5
× 4	× 5	× 6	× 5	× 3	× 8	× 6

5	6	6	4	5	6	3
× 8	× 8	× 6	× 5	× 5	× 5	× 5

6	6	5	5	8	8	4
× 5	× 6	× 5	× 3	× 6	× 5	× 5

6	3	5	8	5	6	5
× 8	× 5	× 4	× 6	× 6	× 6	× 8

Practice **Fives**, **Pretend to Add**, and **Count by 3s**.

5	6	8	6	7	4	3
× 8	× 5	× 8	× 3	× 7	× 5	× 6

5	8	7	5	6	8	3
× 3	× 5	× 7	× 6	× 3	× 8	× 3

5	3	5	5	3	7	6
× 4	× 5	× 6	× 8	× 5	× 7	× 5

8	3	5	3	4	8	5
× 8	× 6	× 3	× 3	× 5	× 5	× 4

Five Times Five Is Not Ten: Make Multiplication Easy **105**

Name _____

REVIEW
Practice **Fives**, **4 Fingers**, and **Count 5, 6, 7, 8**.

$\begin{array}{r} 8 \\ \times 5 \\ \hline \end{array}$	$\begin{array}{r} 7 \\ \times 4 \\ \hline \end{array}$	$\begin{array}{r} 4 \\ \times 4 \\ \hline \end{array}$	$\begin{array}{r} 8 \\ \times 7 \\ \hline \end{array}$	$\begin{array}{r} 5 \\ \times 6 \\ \hline \end{array}$	$\begin{array}{r} 4 \\ \times 3 \\ \hline \end{array}$	$\begin{array}{r} 3 \\ \times 5 \\ \hline \end{array}$
$\begin{array}{r} 3 \\ \times 4 \\ \hline \end{array}$	$\begin{array}{r} 6 \\ \times 5 \\ \hline \end{array}$	$\begin{array}{r} 7 \\ \times 8 \\ \hline \end{array}$	$\begin{array}{r} 5 \\ \times 3 \\ \hline \end{array}$	$\begin{array}{r} 4 \\ \times 5 \\ \hline \end{array}$	$\begin{array}{r} 8 \\ \times 7 \\ \hline \end{array}$	$\begin{array}{r} 6 \\ \times 4 \\ \hline \end{array}$
$\begin{array}{r} 4 \\ \times 7 \\ \hline \end{array}$	$\begin{array}{r} 8 \\ \times 7 \\ \hline \end{array}$	$\begin{array}{r} 3 \\ \times 5 \\ \hline \end{array}$	$\begin{array}{r} 4 \\ \times 6 \\ \hline \end{array}$	$\begin{array}{r} 7 \\ \times 8 \\ \hline \end{array}$	$\begin{array}{r} 5 \\ \times 8 \\ \hline \end{array}$	$\begin{array}{r} 4 \\ \times 4 \\ \hline \end{array}$
$\begin{array}{r} 4 \\ \times 5 \\ \hline \end{array}$	$\begin{array}{r} 6 \\ \times 4 \\ \hline \end{array}$	$\begin{array}{r} 5 \\ \times 6 \\ \hline \end{array}$	$\begin{array}{r} 5 \\ \times 8 \\ \hline \end{array}$	$\begin{array}{r} 7 \\ \times 4 \\ \hline \end{array}$	$\begin{array}{r} 5 \\ \times 4 \\ \hline \end{array}$	$\begin{array}{r} 7 \\ \times 8 \\ \hline \end{array}$

Practice **Fives**, **Doubles**, and **Pretend to Add**.

$5 \times 3 =$ _____	$2 \times 8 =$ _____	$3 \times 2 =$ _____	$6 \times 5 =$ _____
$7 \times 7 =$ _____	$6 \times 2 =$ _____	$8 \times 8 =$ _____	$9 \times 2 =$ _____
$5 \times 8 =$ _____	$5 \times 6 =$ _____	$2 \times 4 =$ _____	$4 \times 5 =$ _____
$8 \times 8 =$ _____	$7 \times 7 =$ _____	$5 \times 8 =$ _____	$2 \times 7 =$ _____
$2 \times 5 =$ _____	$5 \times 4 =$ _____	$3 \times 5 =$ _____	$7 \times 7 =$ _____
$5 \times 6 =$ _____	$2 \times 2 =$ _____	$8 \times 5 =$ _____	$8 \times 8 =$ _____

Name _____

REVIEW
Practice **Pretend to Add**, **1 Group**, and **Rhymes**.

8 × 8	7 × 1	8 × 6	6 × 1	6 × 6	7 × 7	6 × 8
9 × 1	7 × 7	1 × 3	8 × 8	5 × 1	8 × 6	1 × 8
6 × 6	4 × 1	7 × 7	6 × 8	1 × 2	8 × 8	1 × 1
8 × 6	1 × 5	8 × 8	1 × 7	6 × 8	6 × 6	7 × 7

Practice **Pretend to Add**, **See 2 4s**, and **Doubles**.

7 × 7	8 × 3	9 × 2	2 × 6	3 × 8	2 × 4	8 × 8
3 × 8	7 × 2	2 × 8	8 × 8	7 × 7	8 × 3	5 × 2
6 × 2	8 × 8	8 × 3	2 × 5	3 × 8	2 × 2	7 × 7
2 × 7	3 × 8	7 × 7	8 × 3	4 × 2	8 × 8	3 × 2

Five Times Five Is Not Ten: Make Multiplication Easy **107**

Name _____

REVIEW
Practice **4 Fingers** and **Pretend to Add with 9**.

3 × 4	7 × 4	4 × 6	7 × 9	9 × 5	9 × 9	4 × 4
4 × 7	9 × 7	9 × 4	4 × 3	6 × 9	5 × 4	5 × 9
9 × 6	4 × 4	4 × 5	4 × 9	3 × 4	7 × 9	6 × 4
4 × 6	9 × 5	4 × 7	6 × 4	5 × 4	9 × 4	9 × 6

Practice **4 Fingers**, **I See 2 5s**, and **Pretend to Add**.

5×4= _____	3×4= _____	5×5= _____	4×7= _____
8×8= _____	7×7= _____	6×4= _____	4×4= _____
7×4= _____	4×5= _____	4×3= _____	7×7= _____
4×6= _____	8×8= _____	4×4= _____	5×5= _____
7×7= _____	5×5= _____	5×4= _____	7×4= _____
3×4= _____	6×4= _____	8×8= _____	4×5= _____

Five Times Five Is Not Ten: Make Multiplication Easy

Name _____

REVIEW

Practice **See 2 4s**, **I See 2 5s**, and **Count by 3s**.

8 × 3	5 × 5	3 × 6	6 × 3	3 × 8	3 × 3	3 × 8
3 × 3	6 × 3	3 × 8	5 × 5	8 × 3	3 × 6	5 × 5
8 × 3	3 × 3	6 × 3	3 × 8	6 × 3	5 × 5	3 × 3
6 × 3	3 × 8	3 × 3	3 × 6	5 × 5	8 × 3	3 × 6

Practice **See 2 4s**, **Pretend to Add with 9**, and **Count 5,6,7,8**.

8 × 3	9 × 7	7 × 8	9 × 4	5 × 9	8 × 7	3 × 8
9 × 5	8 × 7	9 × 9	6 × 9	8 × 3	9 × 6	7 × 8
7 × 9	3 × 8	8 × 7	5 × 9	7 × 8	3 × 8	4 × 9
9 × 6	9 × 4	8 × 3	8 × 7	9 × 9	9 × 5	7 × 9

Name _____

REVIEW
Practice **Pretend to Add with 9** and **Fives**.

9 × 6	5 × 9	8 × 5	5 × 6	9 × 7	9 × 4	3 × 5
4 × 9	6 × 5	9 × 9	5 × 3	5 × 8	6 × 9	5 × 4
5 × 8	7 × 9	4 × 5	9 × 5	6 × 9	6 × 5	9 × 4
9 × 5	5 × 4	3 × 5	5 × 6	5 × 3	8 × 5	9 × 7

Practice **Pretend to Add with 9**, **Rhymes**, and **Count by 3s**.

7×9= _____   6×8= _____   3×3= _____   6×6= _____

6×3= _____   6×9= _____   9×5= _____   3×6= _____

9×4= _____   9×9= _____   6×6= _____   8×6= _____

8×6= _____   3×3= _____   9×7= _____   4×9= _____

5×9= _____   6×6= _____   6×8= _____   9×6= _____

3×6= _____   6×8= _____   6×3= _____   8×6= _____

Five Times Five Is Not Ten: Make Multiplication Easy

More Fives

You know 6 groups of 5 = **30**.

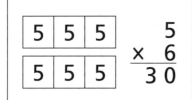

$$\begin{array}{r} 5 \\ \times\ 6 \\ \hline 3\ 0 \end{array}$$

Add on one more 5.

$+\ \boxed{5}$

$$\begin{array}{r} 3\ 0 \\ +\ \mathbf{5} \\ \hline \mathbf{3\ 5} \end{array}$$

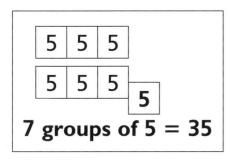

7 groups of 5 = 35

These are the same.

$$\begin{array}{r} 5 \\ \times\ 7 \\ \hline \mathbf{35} \end{array} \qquad \begin{array}{r} 7 \\ \times\ 5 \\ \hline \mathbf{35} \end{array}$$

Practice **Fives**.

$$\begin{array}{r} 5 \\ \times\ 7 \\ \hline \end{array} \quad \begin{array}{r} 4 \\ \times\ 5 \\ \hline \end{array} \quad \begin{array}{r} 5 \\ \times\ 7 \\ \hline \end{array} \quad \begin{array}{r} 3 \\ \times\ 5 \\ \hline \end{array} \quad \begin{array}{r} 7 \\ \times\ 5 \\ \hline \end{array} \quad \begin{array}{r} 5 \\ \times\ 6 \\ \hline \end{array} \quad \begin{array}{r} 7 \\ \times\ 5 \\ \hline \end{array}$$

$$\begin{array}{r} 5 \\ \times\ 8 \\ \hline \end{array} \quad \begin{array}{r} 7 \\ \times\ 5 \\ \hline \end{array} \quad \begin{array}{r} 5 \\ \times\ 3 \\ \hline \end{array} \quad \begin{array}{r} 5 \\ \times\ 6 \\ \hline \end{array} \quad \begin{array}{r} 5 \\ \times\ 4 \\ \hline \end{array} \quad \begin{array}{r} 5 \\ \times\ 7 \\ \hline \end{array} \quad \begin{array}{r} 5 \\ \times\ 3 \\ \hline \end{array}$$

$$\begin{array}{r} 3 \\ \times\ 5 \\ \hline \end{array} \quad \begin{array}{r} 6 \\ \times\ 5 \\ \hline \end{array} \quad \begin{array}{r} 7 \\ \times\ 5 \\ \hline \end{array} \quad \begin{array}{r} 8 \\ \times\ 5 \\ \hline \end{array} \quad \begin{array}{r} 5 \\ \times\ 3 \\ \hline \end{array} \quad \begin{array}{r} 4 \\ \times\ 5 \\ \hline \end{array} \quad \begin{array}{r} 5 \\ \times\ 7 \\ \hline \end{array}$$

$$\begin{array}{r} 8 \\ \times\ 5 \\ \hline \end{array} \quad \begin{array}{r} 5 \\ \times\ 3 \\ \hline \end{array} \quad \begin{array}{r} 6 \\ \times\ 5 \\ \hline \end{array} \quad \begin{array}{r} 5 \\ \times\ 7 \\ \hline \end{array} \quad \begin{array}{r} 5 \\ \times\ 8 \\ \hline \end{array} \quad \begin{array}{r} 7 \\ \times\ 5 \\ \hline \end{array} \quad \begin{array}{r} 5 \\ \times\ 4 \\ \hline \end{array}$$

Name _____

Practice **Fives** and **Count by 3s**.

7 × 5	5 × 6	5 × 7	6 × 3	5 × 8	5 × 7	5 × 4
3 × 6	5 × 7	8 × 5	3 × 5	6 × 3	4 × 5	7 × 5
5 × 3	3 × 3	3 × 6	7 × 5	6 × 5	7 × 5	5 × 8
5 × 7	5 × 4	7 × 5	5 × 6	5 × 7	3 × 3	3 × 5

Practice **Fives**, **Count 5,6,7,8**, and **Doubles**.

5 × 7	9 × 2	5 × 6	7 × 5	8 × 7	2 × 3	5 × 7
5 × 4	7 × 5	7 × 8	2 × 6	5 × 7	8 × 7	7 × 2
5 × 8	2 × 8	7 × 5	4 × 5	5 × 3	5 × 7	2 × 5
8 × 7	3 × 5	4 × 2	8 × 5	6 × 5	7 × 8	7 × 5

Name _____

Practice **Fives**, **Pretend to Add**, and **1 Group**.

5 × 8	7 × 5	1 × 4	8 × 8	5 × 7	3 × 5	3 × 1
5 × 7	6 × 1	5 × 6	5 × 4	7 × 7	1 × 2	7 × 5
1 × 7	8 × 8	7 × 5	8 × 1	1 × 1	5 × 7	6 × 5
7 × 7	5 × 7	1 × 5	8 × 5	4 × 5	1 × 9	5 × 3

Practice **Fives**, **Rhymes**, and **See 2 4s**.

$7 \times 5 =$ _____ $6 \times 8 =$ _____ $4 \times 5 =$ _____ $5 \times 8 =$ _____

$3 \times 8 =$ _____ $5 \times 7 =$ _____ $6 \times 6 =$ _____ $6 \times 5 =$ _____

$8 \times 5 =$ _____ $5 \times 3 =$ _____ $8 \times 3 =$ _____ $7 \times 5 =$ _____

$5 \times 7 =$ _____ $6 \times 6 =$ _____ $8 \times 6 =$ _____ $3 \times 5 =$ _____

$8 \times 3 =$ _____ $7 \times 5 =$ _____ $5 \times 6 =$ _____ $5 \times 7 =$ _____

$6 \times 8 =$ _____ $5 \times 4 =$ _____ $3 \times 8 =$ _____ $8 \times 6 =$ _____

Name _____

Cumulative Practice.

9	7	8	5	0	8	3
$\times\,6$	$\times\,5$	$\times\,2$	$\times\,7$	$\times\,5$	$\times\,6$	$\times\,5$

5	4	7	2	7	4	5
$\times\,5$	$\times\,6$	$\times\,8$	$\times\,6$	$\times\,7$	$\times\,5$	$\times\,7$

4	9	4	8	7	7	8
$\times\,9$	$\times\,9$	$\times\,3$	$\times\,8$	$\times\,5$	$\times\,1$	$\times\,3$

7	2	5	3	4	8	9
$\times\,4$	$\times\,2$	$\times\,7$	$\times\,6$	$\times\,4$	$\times\,5$	$\times\,7$

Practice this way.

$5 \times 7 =$ _____ $6 \times 6 =$ _____ $3 \times 5 =$ _____ $7 \times 1 =$ _____

$5 \times 9 =$ _____ $4 \times 5 =$ _____ $2 \times 3 =$ _____ $7 \times 5 =$ _____

$0 \times 6 =$ _____ $7 \times 8 =$ _____ $7 \times 4 =$ _____ $8 \times 6 =$ _____

$9 \times 6 =$ _____ $5 \times 6 =$ _____ $8 \times 3 =$ _____ $9 \times 5 =$ _____

$5 \times 2 =$ _____ $1 \times 5 =$ _____ $9 \times 7 =$ _____ $8 \times 5 =$ _____

$3 \times 6 =$ _____ $4 \times 6 =$ _____ $5 \times 7 =$ _____ $6 \times 5 =$ _____

More 4 Fingers

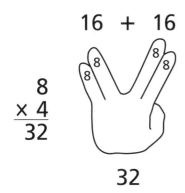

16 + 16

8
× 4
32

32

4 groups of 8

⸺⸺⸺⸺⸺⸺⸺⸺⸺⸺⸺

16   +   16

32

Draw 8 groups of 4.

These are the same.

8	4
× **4**	× **8**
32	32

Practice **4 Fingers** and **Doubles**.

8	4	4	7	8	4	8
× 4	× 8	× 4	× 2	× 4	× 6	× 4

4	4	4	4	7	4	2
× 5	× 2	× 8	× 3	× 4	× 8	× 9

4	6	5	3	4	2	4
× 8	× 4	× 2	× 2	× 4	× 6	× 8

2	5	8	4	2	8	3
× 2	× 4	× 4	× 7	× 8	× 4	× 4

Name _____

Practice **4 Fingers** with addition and subtraction.

8 × 4	4 + 4	4 × 8	4 × 4	8 − 4	6 × 4	4 × 8
7 − 7	8 × 4	4 × 3	8 × 4	4 × 7	4 + 8	4 − 3
5 × 4	6 + 4	4 × 8	5 − 4	4 × 8	3 × 4	8 × 4
7 × 4	4 × 8	8 + 4	4 × 5	8 + 8	8 × 4	4 × 6

Practice **4 Fingers** and **Pretend to Add**.

7 × 4	4 × 8	4 × 6	8 × 4	7 × 7	4 × 4	8 × 4
4 × 8	3 × 4	4 × 5	4 × 6	8 × 8	4 × 8	6 × 4
7 × 7	4 × 7	4 × 8	4 × 3	4 × 4	5 × 4	8 × 8
8 × 4	6 × 4	8 × 8	5 × 4	8 × 4	7 × 7	7 × 4

Name _____

Practice **4 Fingers**, **I See 2 5s**, and **Count by 3s**.

4	4	7	6	8	5	3
× 4	× 8	× 4	× 3	× 4	× 4	× 3

3	6	4	4	4	5	8
× 6	× 4	× 8	× 7	× 3	× 5	× 4

4	8	5	6	3	4	3
× 7	× 4	× 5	× 4	× 6	× 8	× 4

4	3	4	8	5	4	6
× 8	× 3	× 5	× 4	× 5	× 6	× 3

Practice **4 Fingers** and **Pretend to Add with 9**.

4	5	7	6	8	9	4
× 8	× 9	× 4	× 9	× 4	× 7	× 6

7	8	4	4	9	4	4
× 9	× 4	× 3	× 4	× 6	× 8	× 5

4	9	4	5	4	3	8
× 7	× 9	× 9	× 4	× 8	× 4	× 4

4	7	8	6	9	4	9
× 5	× 9	× 4	× 4	× 5	× 8	× 4

Five Times Five Is Not Ten: Make Multiplication Easy

Name _____

Practice **4 Fingers** and **Fives**.

4 × 8	7 × 4	6 × 5	4 × 5	3 × 4	7 × 5	8 × 4
5 × 3	5 × 8	5 × 7	6 × 4	5 × 6	4 × 8	4 × 4
8 × 5	8 × 4	4 × 3	4 × 7	4 × 8	3 × 5	8 × 5
8 × 4	7 × 5	4 × 5	5 × 8	4 × 6	5 × 7	5 × 6

Practice **4 Fingers** and **See 2 4s**.

4 × 7	5 × 4	8 × 3	4 × 6	3 × 8	7 × 4	8 × 4
8 × 3	4 × 3	8 × 4	4 × 5	4 × 8	6 × 4	3 × 8
4 × 4	3 × 8	3 × 4	8 × 3	3 × 4	4 × 8	4 × 7
6 × 4	8 × 4	8 × 3	4 × 8	5 × 4	3 × 8	4 × 6

STRETCH

STRETCH your imagination.

STRETCH **3 × 7 = 2 1**

STRETCH **7 × 3 = 2 1**

Remember that **3 × 7** and **7 × 3 = 21**.

Practice **STRETCH** and **4 Fingers**. (Circle) **STRETCH**.

7 × 3	4 × 7	8 × 4	7 × 3	3 × 7	4 × 4	3 × 7
6 × 4	4 × 8	3 × 7	5 × 4	7 × 4	7 × 3	8 × 4
3 × 7	3 × 4	8 × 4	3 × 7	4 × 6	4 × 7	7 × 3
4 × 5	7 × 3	4 × 4	4 × 8	7 × 3	4 × 3	4 × 8

Name _____

Practice **STRETCH**, **I See 2 5s**, and **Fives**.

3 × 7	5 × 5	7 × 3	5 × 6	8 × 5	3 × 7	3 × 5
6 × 5	7 × 3	5 × 4	3 × 7	5 × 7	5 × 5	7 × 3
3 × 7	5 × 8	5 × 3	7 × 3	3 × 7	7 × 5	4 × 5
5 × 5	5 × 3	5 × 6	7 × 5	5 × 5	3 × 7	5 × 8

Practice **STRETCH**, **1 Group**, and **Pretend to Add with 9**.

7 × 3	7 × 9	9 × 6	3 × 7	7 × 1	7 × 3	5 × 9
3 × 1	3 × 7	1 × 1	4 × 9	7 × 3	1 × 8	9 × 1
9 × 9	1 × 7	7 × 3	9 × 5	9 × 7	3 × 7	5 × 1
3 × 7	9 × 4	1 × 6	7 × 3	1 × 3	6 × 9	7 × 3

Name _____

Practice **STRETCH**, **Rhymes**, and **See 2 4s**.

7 × 3	3 × 8	8 × 6	3 × 7	6 × 8	6 × 6	3 × 7
3 × 8	6 × 6	7 × 3	6 × 8	8 × 3	7 × 3	3 × 8
8 × 6	3 × 7	8 × 3	3 × 8	7 × 3	6 × 8	6 × 6
8 × 3	6 × 8	3 × 7	7 × 3	8 × 6	3 × 7	8 × 3

Practice **STRETCH**, **Count 5, 6, 7, 8**, and **Count by 3s**. ⃝Circle **STRETCH**.

3 × 7	8 × 7	7 × 3	3 × 3	6 × 3	3 × 7	7 × 8
3 × 6	7 × 3	7 × 8	3 × 6	3 × 7	3 × 3	7 × 3
8 × 7	7 × 8	3 × 7	3 × 3	6 × 3	8 × 7	3 × 6
6 × 3	3 × 7	8 × 7	7 × 3	7 × 8	7 × 3	3 × 3

Five Times Five Is Not Ten: Make Multiplication Easy **121**

Name _____

Practice **STRETCH** and **Zero** with addition and subtraction.

$$\begin{array}{r} 7 \\ \times\, 3 \\ \hline \end{array} \qquad \begin{array}{r} 7 \\ +\, 3 \\ \hline \end{array} \qquad \begin{array}{r} 0 \\ \times\, 7 \\ \hline \end{array} \qquad \begin{array}{r} 3 \\ \times\, 7 \\ \hline \end{array} \qquad \begin{array}{r} 7 \\ -\, 7 \\ \hline \end{array} \qquad \begin{array}{r} 7 \\ \times\, 3 \\ \hline \end{array} \qquad \begin{array}{r} 3 \\ \times\, 0 \\ \hline \end{array}$$

$$\begin{array}{r} 5 \\ \times\, 0 \\ \hline \end{array} \qquad \begin{array}{r} 7 \\ -\, 0 \\ \hline \end{array} \qquad \begin{array}{r} 3 \\ +\, 0 \\ \hline \end{array} \qquad \begin{array}{r} 0 \\ \times\, 3 \\ \hline \end{array} \qquad \begin{array}{r} 3 \\ \times\, 7 \\ \hline \end{array} \qquad \begin{array}{r} 3 \\ -\, 0 \\ \hline \end{array} \qquad \begin{array}{r} 7 \\ \times\, 3 \\ \hline \end{array}$$

$$\begin{array}{r} 0 \\ +\, 7 \\ \hline \end{array} \qquad \begin{array}{r} 0 \\ \times\, 4 \\ \hline \end{array} \qquad \begin{array}{r} 7 \\ \times\, 3 \\ \hline \end{array} \qquad \begin{array}{r} 0 \\ \times\, 6 \\ \hline \end{array} \qquad \begin{array}{r} 0 \\ +\, 3 \\ \hline \end{array} \qquad \begin{array}{r} 3 \\ \times\, 7 \\ \hline \end{array} \qquad \begin{array}{r} 7 \\ +\, 0 \\ \hline \end{array}$$

$$\begin{array}{r} 3 \\ \times\, 7 \\ \hline \end{array} \qquad \begin{array}{r} 9 \\ \times\, 0 \\ \hline \end{array} \qquad \begin{array}{r} 7 \\ \times\, 0 \\ \hline \end{array} \qquad \begin{array}{r} 3 \\ +\, 7 \\ \hline \end{array} \qquad \begin{array}{r} 3 \\ -\, 3 \\ \hline \end{array} \qquad \begin{array}{r} 0 \\ \times\, 1 \\ \hline \end{array} \qquad \begin{array}{r} 0 \\ \times\, 8 \\ \hline \end{array}$$

Practice **STRETCH**, **Doubles**, and **Pretend to Add**.

$3 \times 7 =$ _____ $3 \times 2 =$ _____ $7 \times 3 =$ _____ $8 \times 8 =$ _____

$2 \times 9 =$ _____ $7 \times 3 =$ _____ $7 \times 7 =$ _____ $2 \times 4 =$ _____

$7 \times 7 =$ _____ $2 \times 7 =$ _____ $5 \times 2 =$ _____ $3 \times 7 =$ _____

$6 \times 2 =$ _____ $8 \times 8 =$ _____ $3 \times 7 =$ _____ $2 \times 3 =$ _____

$7 \times 3 =$ _____ $7 \times 7 =$ _____ $7 \times 2 =$ _____ $2 \times 8 =$ _____

$8 \times 8 =$ _____ $3 \times 7 =$ _____ $8 \times 8 =$ _____ $7 \times 3 =$ _____

Name _____

Cumulative Practice.

5	3	4	3	7	5	6
× 5	× 7	× 6	× 2	× 3	× 8	× 6

8	8	7	9	1	8	3
× 4	× 6	× 3	× 4	× 5	× 3	× 7

7	0	7	3	9	4	9
× 7	× 3	× 9	× 7	× 5	× 7	× 6

3	5	4	5	8	7	4
× 8	× 9	× 4	× 3	× 8	× 8	× 3

Practice this way.

8×4= _____   1×4= _____   8×6= _____   5×7= _____

7×9= _____   6×5= _____   3×3= _____   0×7= _____

3×7= _____   4×5= _____   9×9= _____   4×7= _____

5×8= _____   8×2= _____   7×3= _____   9×4= _____

4×6= _____   7×5= _____   6×3= _____   5×6= _____

2×2= _____   3×7= _____   9×6= _____   7×8= _____

Name _____

Cumulative Practice.

8 × 6	4 × 9	3 × 4	2 × 7	8 × 4	8 × 8	3 × 7
3 × 5	3 × 8	4 × 0	9 × 5	5 × 7	4 × 6	6 × 6
7 × 3	7 × 4	4 × 5	7 × 9	2 × 9	7 × 7	5 × 3
9 × 6	9 × 1	3 × 7	4 × 4	6 × 5	3 × 3	7 × 8
7 × 3	9 × 9	4 × 8	7 × 5	0 × 2	3 × 7	6 × 3
5 × 5	8 × 5	5 × 4	7 × 3	4 × 7	4 × 3	9 × 4
8 × 7	8 × 3	6 × 4	6 × 2	5 × 9	5 × 6	6 × 9
4 × 2	3 × 7	3 × 6	6 × 8	9 × 7	7 × 3	5 × 8

Five Times Five Is Not Ten: Make Multiplication Easy

Think of 7 × 7

You know
$$\begin{array}{r} 7 \\ \times\ 7 \\ \hline 49 \end{array}$$

7 groups of 7

| 7 | 7 | 7 | 7 | 7 | 7 | ⟨7⟩ |

$$\begin{array}{r} 49 \\ -\ 7 \\ \hline 42 \end{array}$$ Take away one 7.

Now you have

| 7 | 7 | 7 | 7 | 7 | 7 |

6 groups of 7.

$$\begin{array}{r} 7 \\ \times\ 6 \\ \hline 42 \end{array}$$

You know STRETCH: 3×7 and 7×3.

3 groups of 7 = 21 | 7 | 7 | 7 | and | 7 | 7 | 7 |

21   +   21   = 42

These are the same.

$$\begin{array}{cc} \begin{array}{r} 7 \\ \times\ 6 \\ \hline \mathbf{42} \end{array} & \begin{array}{r} 6 \\ \times\ 7 \\ \hline \mathbf{42} \end{array} \end{array}$$

Practice **Think of 7 × 7** and **Pretend to Add**.

6×7= _____   7×7= _____   7×6= _____   8×8= _____

7×7= _____   7×6= _____   7×7= _____   6×7= _____

7×6= _____   8×8= _____   6×7= _____   7×7= _____

8×8= _____   6×7= _____   8×8= _____   7×6= _____

Name _____

Practice **Think of 7 × 7**, **Pretend to Add**, and **STRETCH**.

6 × 7	7 × 7	7 × 6	7 × 3	6 × 7	7 × 7	3 × 7
8 × 8	7 × 6	7 × 3	7 × 7	8 × 8	6 × 7	7 × 7
7 × 6	7 × 3	6 × 7	3 × 7	6 × 7	8 × 8	7 × 6
3 × 7	8 × 8	7 × 7	7 × 6	7 × 3	3 × 7	8 × 8

Practice **Think of 7 × 7**, **Pretend to Add**, and **Fives**.

7 × 6	6 × 5	7 × 7	6 × 7	8 × 8	5 × 4	6 × 7
8 × 5	7 × 6	3 × 5	7 × 7	6 × 7	7 × 6	8 × 8
7 × 7	5 × 7	6 × 7	5 × 6	5 × 8	7 × 5	7 × 6
5 × 3	6 × 7	8 × 8	8 × 5	7 × 6	5 × 7	4 × 5

Five Times Five Is Not Ten: Make Multiplication Easy

Name _____

Practice **Think of 7 × 7** and **4 Fingers**.

6 × 7	8 × 4	6 × 4	7 × 6	4 × 3	6 × 7	4 × 6
5 × 4	7 × 6	4 × 8	4 × 4	7 × 6	4 × 5	3 × 4
4 × 7	4 × 4	6 × 7	4 × 5	4 × 8	7 × 6	7 × 4
4 × 3	6 × 7	7 × 4	7 × 6	6 × 4	8 × 4	6 × 7

Practice **Think of 7 × 7**, **See 2 4s**, and **Pretend to Add with 9**.

6 × 7	7 × 9	9 × 4	7 × 6	8 × 3	9 × 6	9 × 5
3 × 8	4 × 9	7 × 6	9 × 5	6 × 9	6 × 7	8 × 3
9 × 9	6 × 7	7 × 9	3 × 8	7 × 6	4 × 9	7 × 6
9 × 6	8 × 3	5 × 9	6 × 7	9 × 9	3 × 8	9 × 7

Name _____

Practice **Think of 7 × 7**, **Rhymes**, and **I See 2 5s**.

$\begin{array}{r} 7 \\ \times\,6 \\ \hline \end{array}$	$\begin{array}{r} 8 \\ \times\,6 \\ \hline \end{array}$	$\begin{array}{r} 6 \\ \times\,6 \\ \hline \end{array}$	$\begin{array}{r} 5 \\ \times\,5 \\ \hline \end{array}$	$\begin{array}{r} 6 \\ \times\,7 \\ \hline \end{array}$	$\begin{array}{r} 8 \\ \times\,6 \\ \hline \end{array}$	$\begin{array}{r} 6 \\ \times\,8 \\ \hline \end{array}$
$\begin{array}{r} 5 \\ \times\,5 \\ \hline \end{array}$	$\begin{array}{r} 6 \\ \times\,7 \\ \hline \end{array}$	$\begin{array}{r} 6 \\ \times\,8 \\ \hline \end{array}$	$\begin{array}{r} 7 \\ \times\,6 \\ \hline \end{array}$	$\begin{array}{r} 8 \\ \times\,6 \\ \hline \end{array}$	$\begin{array}{r} 6 \\ \times\,6 \\ \hline \end{array}$	$\begin{array}{r} 6 \\ \times\,7 \\ \hline \end{array}$
$\begin{array}{r} 8 \\ \times\,6 \\ \hline \end{array}$	$\begin{array}{r} 6 \\ \times\,6 \\ \hline \end{array}$	$\begin{array}{r} 6 \\ \times\,7 \\ \hline \end{array}$	$\begin{array}{r} 6 \\ \times\,8 \\ \hline \end{array}$	$\begin{array}{r} 5 \\ \times\,5 \\ \hline \end{array}$	$\begin{array}{r} 7 \\ \times\,6 \\ \hline \end{array}$	$\begin{array}{r} 6 \\ \times\,6 \\ \hline \end{array}$
$\begin{array}{r} 6 \\ \times\,7 \\ \hline \end{array}$	$\begin{array}{r} 8 \\ \times\,6 \\ \hline \end{array}$	$\begin{array}{r} 5 \\ \times\,5 \\ \hline \end{array}$	$\begin{array}{r} 6 \\ \times\,6 \\ \hline \end{array}$	$\begin{array}{r} 7 \\ \times\,6 \\ \hline \end{array}$	$\begin{array}{r} 6 \\ \times\,8 \\ \hline \end{array}$	$\begin{array}{r} 7 \\ \times\,6 \\ \hline \end{array}$

Practice **Think of 7 × 7**, **Count by 3s**, and **Doubles**.

7×6= _____   8×2= _____   6×3= _____   6×7= _____

2×3= _____   6×7= _____   3×3= _____   2×7= _____

3×6= _____   7×6= _____   5×2= _____   3×3= _____

6×7= _____   6×3= _____   7×6= _____   3×6= _____

6×3= _____   2×4= _____   3×6= _____   7×6= _____

6×2= _____   3×3= _____   6×7= _____   9×2= _____

Name _____

More Pretend to Add with 9

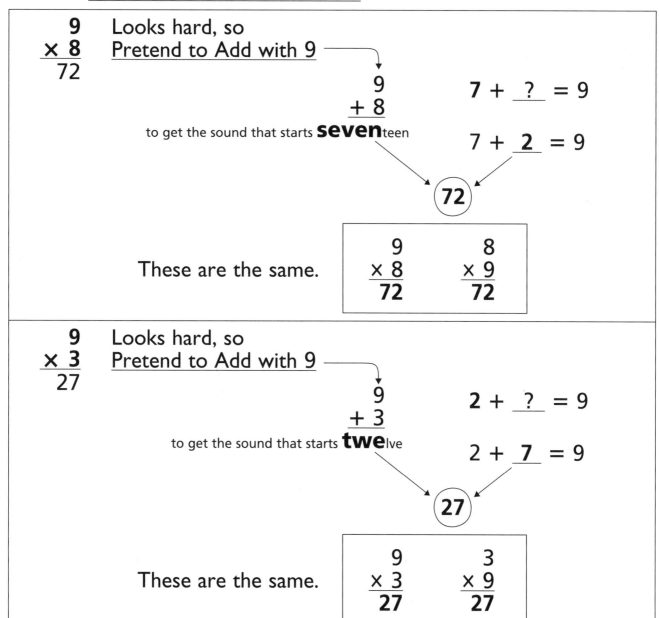

$$\begin{array}{r} 9 \\ \times\ 8 \\ \hline 72 \end{array}$$

Looks hard, so
Pretend to Add with 9

$$\begin{array}{r} 9 \\ +\ 8 \end{array}$$

to get the sound that starts **seven**teen

$7 + \underline{\ ?\ } = 9$

$7 + \underline{\ 2\ } = 9$

72

These are the same.

$$\begin{array}{r} 9 \\ \times\ 8 \\ \hline 72 \end{array} \qquad \begin{array}{r} 8 \\ \times\ 9 \\ \hline 72 \end{array}$$

$$\begin{array}{r} 9 \\ \times\ 3 \\ \hline 27 \end{array}$$

Looks hard, so
Pretend to Add with 9

$$\begin{array}{r} 9 \\ +\ 3 \end{array}$$

to get the sound that starts **twe**lve

$2 + \underline{\ ?\ } = 9$

$2 + \underline{\ 7\ } = 9$

27

These are the same.

$$\begin{array}{r} 9 \\ \times\ 3 \\ \hline 27 \end{array} \qquad \begin{array}{r} 3 \\ \times\ 9 \\ \hline 27 \end{array}$$

Practice **Pretend to Add with 9**.

$$\begin{array}{r} 8 \\ \times\ 9 \end{array} \qquad \begin{array}{r} 9 \\ \times\ 8 \end{array} \qquad \begin{array}{r} 9 \\ \times\ 3 \end{array} \qquad \begin{array}{r} 3 \\ \times\ 9 \end{array} \qquad \begin{array}{r} 5 \\ \times\ 9 \end{array} \qquad \begin{array}{r} 9 \\ \times\ 8 \end{array} \qquad \begin{array}{r} 3 \\ \times\ 9 \end{array}$$

$$\begin{array}{r} 9 \\ \times\ 7 \end{array} \qquad \begin{array}{r} 9 \\ \times\ 3 \end{array} \qquad \begin{array}{r} 8 \\ \times\ 9 \end{array} \qquad \begin{array}{r} 9 \\ \times\ 4 \end{array} \qquad \begin{array}{r} 3 \\ \times\ 9 \end{array} \qquad \begin{array}{r} 9 \\ \times\ 6 \end{array} \qquad \begin{array}{r} 9 \\ \times\ 8 \end{array}$$

Name _____

Practice **Pretend to Add with 9** and **Count by 3s**.

9 × 8	3 × 3	3 × 9	6 × 3	9 × 3	6 × 9	9 × 8
9 × 7	9 × 3	8 × 9	3 × 9	9 × 9	4 × 9	3 × 6
6 × 3	5 × 9	9 × 3	9 × 8	3 × 6	3 × 3	8 × 9
9 × 3	8 × 9	9 × 6	3 × 6	9 × 8	6 × 3	3 × 9

Practice **Pretend to Add with 9** with addition.

$9 \times 8 =$ _____	$9 + 7 =$ _____	$9 \times 3 =$ _____	$8 \times 9 =$ _____
$5 \times 9 =$ _____	$3 \times 9 =$ _____	$4 + 9 =$ _____	$9 \times 7 =$ _____
$9 + 8 =$ _____	$8 \times 9 =$ _____	$9 + 3 =$ _____	$3 \times 9 =$ _____
$9 \times 9 =$ _____	$5 + 9 =$ _____	$9 \times 8 =$ _____	$9 \times 5 =$ _____
$3 \times 9 =$ _____	$4 \times 9 =$ _____	$9 + 6 =$ _____	$8 + 9 =$ _____
$3 + 9 =$ _____	$6 \times 9 =$ _____	$9 \times 3 =$ _____	$9 \times 8 =$ _____

Five Times Five Is Not Ten: Make Multiplication Easy

Name _____

Practice **Pretend to Add with 9** and **Think of 7 × 7**.

3 × 9	9 × 6	8 × 9	7 × 6	6 × 7	9 × 5	9 × 8

7 × 6	9 × 3	6 × 7	8 × 9	4 × 9	7 × 6	9 × 3

9 × 4	6 × 7	7 × 9	3 × 9	7 × 6	9 × 8	6 × 9

6 × 7	9 × 8	9 × 3	5 × 9	9 × 7	3 × 9	8 × 9

Practice **Pretend to Add with 9** and **Count 5,6,7,8**.

8×9= _____	7×8= _____	9×8= _____	6×9= _____
9×3= _____	8×9= _____	3×9= _____	8×7= _____
5×9= _____	8×7= _____	9×4= _____	9×3= _____
7×8= _____	9×8= _____	9×9= _____	3×9= _____
4×9= _____	9×3= _____	8×7= _____	9×8= _____
3×9= _____	9×7= _____	8×9= _____	7×8= _____

Five Times Five Is Not Ten: Make Multiplication Easy **131**

Name _____

Practice **Pretend to Add with 9** and **STRETCH**.

9 × 3	8 × 9	7 × 3	5 × 9	3 × 9	9 × 6	3 × 7
9 × 4	3 × 7	9 × 9	9 × 8	9 × 7	3 × 7	9 × 3
9 × 8	6 × 9	3 × 9	4 × 9	7 × 3	9 × 5	8 × 9
7 × 3	3 × 9	8 × 9	3 × 7	9 × 8	9 × 3	7 × 3

Practice **Pretend to Add with 9** and **See 2 4s**.

9 × 8	9 × 3	9 × 5	8 × 3	7 × 9	8 × 9	3 × 9
6 × 9	3 × 9	3 × 8	9 × 9	9 × 8	9 × 4	8 × 3
8 × 9	8 × 3	4 × 9	8 × 9	3 × 9	9 × 3	9 × 7
3 × 8	7 × 9	9 × 8	9 × 3	5 × 9	9 × 6	3 × 8

Name _____

REVIEW

Practice **Think of 7×7**, **Zero**, and **Count by 3s**.

6 × 7	3 × 3	7 × 6	4 × 0	3 × 6	7 × 6	0 × 7
3 × 6	1 × 0	0 × 9	3 × 3	6 × 7	3 × 0	6 × 3
0 × 5	6 × 3	2 × 0	7 × 6	0 × 0	3 × 6	6 × 7
3 × 3	7 × 6	6 × 3	8 × 0	0 × 6	6 × 7	3 × 6

Practice **Think of 7×7**, **Pretend to Add**, and **I See 2 5s**.

6×7= _____   8×8= _____   7×7= _____   7×6= _____

5×5= _____   7×6= _____   6×7= _____   8×8= _____

7×7= _____   5×5= _____   8×8= _____   6×7= _____

8×8= _____   6×7= _____   7×6= _____   7×7= _____

7×6= _____   5×5= _____   7×7= _____   6×7= _____

8×8= _____   7×6= _____   6×7= _____   5×5= _____

Name _____

REVIEW
Practice **Think of 7×7**, **Count 5,6,7,8**, and **Rhymes**.

7 × 6	6 × 7	8 × 6	6 × 6	8 × 7	6 × 8	7 × 8
6 × 6	6 × 8	6 × 7	8 × 7	7 × 6	7 × 8	6 × 7
7 × 8	7 × 6	8 × 7	6 × 6	8 × 6	6 × 7	6 × 8
8 × 6	6 × 6	7 × 6	6 × 8	7 × 8	8 × 6	8 × 7

Practice **Think of 7×7**, **4 Fingers**, and **See 2 4s**.

7×6= _____	3×8= _____	7×4= _____	3×4= _____
6×7= _____	4×5= _____	6×4= _____	4×8= _____
4×4= _____	7×6= _____	8×3= _____	5×4= _____
4×6= _____	8×4= _____	4×3= _____	6×7= _____
8×3= _____	4×7= _____	4×8= _____	7×4= _____
7×6= _____	6×4= _____	6×7= _____	3×8= _____

Name _____

REVIEW
Practice **Think of 7 × 7**, **STRETCH**, and **1 Group**.

6 × 7	3 × 7	7 × 1	7 × 6	7 × 3	1 × 3	7 × 3
7 × 6	1 × 1	7 × 3	8 × 1	3 × 7	1 × 7	6 × 7
1 × 2	7 × 3	6 × 7	3 × 7	9 × 1	7 × 6	3 × 7
6 × 7	1 × 4	3 × 7	1 × 5	7 × 6	7 × 3	6 × 1

Practice **Think of 7 × 7**, **STRETCH**, and **Doubles**.

$6 \times 7 =$ _____ $3 \times 7 =$ _____ $9 \times 2 =$ _____ $7 \times 3 =$ _____

$8 \times 2 =$ _____ $2 \times 5 =$ _____ $7 \times 6 =$ _____ $2 \times 6 =$ _____

$2 \times 2 =$ _____ $7 \times 3 =$ _____ $4 \times 2 =$ _____ $2 \times 7 =$ _____

$7 \times 3 =$ _____ $2 \times 8 =$ _____ $6 \times 7 =$ _____ $3 \times 7 =$ _____

$7 \times 6 =$ _____ $3 \times 7 =$ _____ $2 \times 3 =$ _____ $6 \times 7 =$ _____

$2 \times 9 =$ _____ $7 \times 6 =$ _____ $7 \times 2 =$ _____ $6 \times 2 =$ _____

Name _____

REVIEW
Practice **Think of 7 × 7**, **STRETCH**, and **Pretend to Add with 9**.

$\begin{array}{r}7\\ \times\,6\\ \hline\end{array}$	$\begin{array}{r}8\\ \times\,9\\ \hline\end{array}$	$\begin{array}{r}7\\ \times\,3\\ \hline\end{array}$	$\begin{array}{r}3\\ \times\,7\\ \hline\end{array}$	$\begin{array}{r}7\\ \times\,6\\ \hline\end{array}$	$\begin{array}{r}4\\ \times\,9\\ \hline\end{array}$	$\begin{array}{r}6\\ \times\,7\\ \hline\end{array}$
$\begin{array}{r}7\\ \times\,3\\ \hline\end{array}$	$\begin{array}{r}9\\ \times\,5\\ \hline\end{array}$	$\begin{array}{r}6\\ \times\,7\\ \hline\end{array}$	$\begin{array}{r}3\\ \times\,9\\ \hline\end{array}$	$\begin{array}{r}9\\ \times\,6\\ \hline\end{array}$	$\begin{array}{r}3\\ \times\,7\\ \hline\end{array}$	$\begin{array}{r}8\\ \times\,9\\ \hline\end{array}$
$\begin{array}{r}9\\ \times\,3\\ \hline\end{array}$	$\begin{array}{r}3\\ \times\,7\\ \hline\end{array}$	$\begin{array}{r}5\\ \times\,9\\ \hline\end{array}$	$\begin{array}{r}9\\ \times\,8\\ \hline\end{array}$	$\begin{array}{r}9\\ \times\,3\\ \hline\end{array}$	$\begin{array}{r}6\\ \times\,7\\ \hline\end{array}$	$\begin{array}{r}9\\ \times\,9\\ \hline\end{array}$
$\begin{array}{r}8\\ \times\,9\\ \hline\end{array}$	$\begin{array}{r}6\\ \times\,7\\ \hline\end{array}$	$\begin{array}{r}3\\ \times\,9\\ \hline\end{array}$	$\begin{array}{r}9\\ \times\,4\\ \hline\end{array}$	$\begin{array}{r}6\\ \times\,7\\ \hline\end{array}$	$\begin{array}{r}6\\ \times\,9\\ \hline\end{array}$	$\begin{array}{r}7\\ \times\,3\\ \hline\end{array}$

Practice **Think of 7 × 7**, **STRETCH**, and **See 2 4s**.

$\begin{array}{r}7\\ \times\,6\\ \hline\end{array}$	$\begin{array}{r}3\\ \times\,7\\ \hline\end{array}$	$\begin{array}{r}8\\ \times\,3\\ \hline\end{array}$	$\begin{array}{r}6\\ \times\,7\\ \hline\end{array}$	$\begin{array}{r}3\\ \times\,8\\ \hline\end{array}$	$\begin{array}{r}7\\ \times\,6\\ \hline\end{array}$	$\begin{array}{r}7\\ \times\,3\\ \hline\end{array}$
$\begin{array}{r}3\\ \times\,8\\ \hline\end{array}$	$\begin{array}{r}8\\ \times\,3\\ \hline\end{array}$	$\begin{array}{r}7\\ \times\,6\\ \hline\end{array}$	$\begin{array}{r}3\\ \times\,7\\ \hline\end{array}$	$\begin{array}{r}7\\ \times\,6\\ \hline\end{array}$	$\begin{array}{r}8\\ \times\,3\\ \hline\end{array}$	$\begin{array}{r}6\\ \times\,7\\ \hline\end{array}$
$\begin{array}{r}7\\ \times\,3\\ \hline\end{array}$	$\begin{array}{r}6\\ \times\,7\\ \hline\end{array}$	$\begin{array}{r}3\\ \times\,8\\ \hline\end{array}$	$\begin{array}{r}7\\ \times\,6\\ \hline\end{array}$	$\begin{array}{r}3\\ \times\,8\\ \hline\end{array}$	$\begin{array}{r}7\\ \times\,3\\ \hline\end{array}$	$\begin{array}{r}3\\ \times\,7\\ \hline\end{array}$
$\begin{array}{r}6\\ \times\,7\\ \hline\end{array}$	$\begin{array}{r}3\\ \times\,8\\ \hline\end{array}$	$\begin{array}{r}7\\ \times\,3\\ \hline\end{array}$	$\begin{array}{r}8\\ \times\,3\\ \hline\end{array}$	$\begin{array}{r}6\\ \times\,7\\ \hline\end{array}$	$\begin{array}{r}3\\ \times\,7\\ \hline\end{array}$	$\begin{array}{r}8\\ \times\,3\\ \hline\end{array}$

Five Times Five Is Not Ten: Make Multiplication Easy

Name _____

REVIEW
Practice **Fives**, **Zero**, and **See 2 4s**.

5 × 3	3 × 8	0 × 6	5 × 7	6 × 5	0 × 3	5 × 7
9 × 0	5 × 8	8 × 3	3 × 5	7 × 5	3 × 8	0 × 2
8 × 3	7 × 5	4 × 5	8 × 0	5 × 3	5 × 6	3 × 8
0 × 7	5 × 4	7 × 5	5 × 7	8 × 3	5 × 0	8 × 5

Practice **Fives**, **Think of 7 × 7**, and **Pretend to Add**.

7×5= _____	5×3= _____	6×7= _____	6×5= _____
7×7= _____	5×6= _____	8×8= _____	7×6= _____
8×5= _____	5×7= _____	5×8= _____	4×5= _____
8×8= _____	7×7= _____	5×7= _____	6×7= _____
5×4= _____	7×6= _____	3×5= _____	7×7= _____
5×6= _____	5×3= _____	7×5= _____	8×8= _____

Name _____

REVIEW

Practice **Fives** and **Rhymes**.

5 × 7	5 × 6	8 × 6	8 × 5	5 × 3	6 × 6	7 × 5
5 × 8	6 × 8	4 × 5	6 × 8	5 × 6	5 × 4	3 × 5
6 × 5	6 × 6	7 × 5	6 × 6	8 × 6	8 × 5	4 × 5
6 × 8	5 × 4	3 × 5	5 × 7	6 × 5	5 × 7	5 × 8

Practice **Fives**, **STRETCH**, and **Count by 3s**.

5 × 3	3 × 7	3 × 6	6 × 3	5 × 8	7 × 3	3 × 3
4 × 5	6 × 3	3 × 7	7 × 5	7 × 3	5 × 7	8 × 5
7 × 3	6 × 5	3 × 3	3 × 6	3 × 5	3 × 7	5 × 4
6 × 3	7 × 3	5 × 7	3 × 7	7 × 5	5 × 6	3 × 6

Five Times Five Is Not Ten: Make Multiplication Easy

Name _____

REVIEW
Practice **STRETCH**, **1 Group**, and **Rhymes**.

7	9	6	8	3	1	8
× 3	× 1	× 6	× 6	× 7	× 7	× 1

8	6	3	2	6	7	8
× 6	× 6	× 7	× 1	× 8	× 3	× 6

1	6	1	3	6	6	7
× 5	× 8	× 4	× 7	× 6	× 8	× 3

6	3	7	6	6	8	3
× 6	× 7	× 3	× 8	× 1	× 6	× 1

Practice **STRETCH**, **I See 2 5s**, and **Pretend to Add**.

7×3= _____   5×5= _____   3×7= _____   8×8= _____

7×7= _____   8×8= _____   5×5= _____   7×3= _____

8×8= _____   3×7= _____   8×8= _____   7×7= _____

3×7= _____   7×7= _____   7×3= _____   3×7= _____

5×5= _____   8×8= _____   3×7= _____   5×5= _____

7×7= _____   7×3= _____   5×5= _____   7×7= _____

Five Times Five Is Not Ten: Make Multiplication Easy

Name _____

REVIEW
Practice **STRETCH**, **I See 2 5s**, and **Count 5,6,7,8**.

3 × 7	5 × 5	7 × 8	7 × 3	5 × 5	8 × 7	7 × 8
5 × 5	7 × 8	7 × 3	8 × 7	3 × 7	5 × 5	7 × 3
8 × 7	3 × 7	5 × 5	7 × 3	7 × 8	3 × 7	8 × 7
7 × 3	8 × 7	3 × 7	5 × 5	3 × 7	7 × 8	5 × 5

Practice **STRETCH**, **See 2 4s**, and **Count by 3s**.

$3 \times 7 =$ _____ $3 \times 3 =$ _____ $3 \times 6 =$ _____ $3 \times 8 =$ _____

$8 \times 3 =$ _____ $6 \times 3 =$ _____ $3 \times 7 =$ _____ $3 \times 3 =$ _____

$7 \times 3 =$ _____ $8 \times 3 =$ _____ $7 \times 3 =$ _____ $3 \times 8 =$ _____

$6 \times 3 =$ _____ $3 \times 7 =$ _____ $6 \times 3 =$ _____ $7 \times 3 =$ _____

$3 \times 8 =$ _____ $3 \times 3 =$ _____ $3 \times 7 =$ _____ $3 \times 6 =$ _____

$3 \times 3 =$ _____ $7 \times 3 =$ _____ $3 \times 6 =$ _____ $8 \times 3 =$ _____

REVIEW
Practice **4 Fingers**, **Pretend to Add**, and **Think of 7 × 7**.

4 × 8	7 × 7	7 × 6	4 × 6	6 × 7	6 × 4	5 × 4
8 × 8	6 × 7	7 × 7	4 × 7	8 × 4	3 × 4	7 × 6
4 × 3	8 × 4	8 × 8	6 × 7	7 × 7	4 × 4	8 × 8
4 × 5	4 × 6	4 × 7	4 × 8	7 × 6	7 × 7	7 × 4

Practice **4 Fingers**, **Fives**, and **Count 5, 6, 7, 8**.

7 × 4	8 × 5	4 × 4	8 × 7	6 × 4	4 × 3	3 × 5
4 × 8	6 × 5	4 × 7	5 × 7	4 × 5	8 × 7	8 × 4
4 × 6	8 × 7	5 × 3	4 × 6	7 × 8	5 × 8	3 × 4
7 × 5	4 × 8	5 × 6	7 × 8	8 × 4	5 × 4	4 × 7

Five Times Five Is Not Ten: Make Multiplication Easy **141**

Name _____

REVIEW
Practice **4 Fingers** and **Pretend to Add with 9**.

8 × 4	9 × 9	4 × 6	8 × 9	9 × 5	3 × 4	4 × 4
4 × 7	9 × 7	9 × 4	9 × 3	6 × 9	5 × 4	5 × 9
9 × 8	4 × 4	4 × 5	4 × 9	7 × 9	3 × 9	6 × 4
4 × 3	8 × 9	4 × 7	4 × 8	9 × 3	7 × 4	9 × 6

Practice **4 Fingers**, **Think of 7 × 7**, and **STRETCH**.

4 × 4	7 × 6	6 × 7	6 × 4	3 × 7	8 × 4	7 × 3
6 × 7	3 × 4	3 × 7	7 × 4	7 × 6	4 × 3	4 × 7
7 × 3	4 × 8	6 × 4	3 × 7	4 × 5	6 × 7	4 × 6
4 × 7	3 × 7	7 × 6	4 × 4	3 × 4	7 × 3	4 × 8

Name _____

REVIEW
Practice **Pretend to Add with 9**, **See 2 4s**, and **Doubles**.

$\begin{array}{r}7\\ \times\,9\\\hline\end{array}$	$\begin{array}{r}8\\ \times\,3\\\hline\end{array}$	$\begin{array}{r}9\\ \times\,2\\\hline\end{array}$	$\begin{array}{r}2\\ \times\,6\\\hline\end{array}$	$\begin{array}{r}3\\ \times\,8\\\hline\end{array}$	$\begin{array}{r}2\\ \times\,4\\\hline\end{array}$	$\begin{array}{r}9\\ \times\,4\\\hline\end{array}$
$\begin{array}{r}8\\ \times\,2\\\hline\end{array}$	$\begin{array}{r}8\\ \times\,9\\\hline\end{array}$	$\begin{array}{r}7\\ \times\,2\\\hline\end{array}$	$\begin{array}{r}6\\ \times\,9\\\hline\end{array}$	$\begin{array}{r}9\\ \times\,3\\\hline\end{array}$	$\begin{array}{r}8\\ \times\,3\\\hline\end{array}$	$\begin{array}{r}5\\ \times\,9\\\hline\end{array}$
$\begin{array}{r}9\\ \times\,5\\\hline\end{array}$	$\begin{array}{r}6\\ \times\,2\\\hline\end{array}$	$\begin{array}{r}9\\ \times\,7\\\hline\end{array}$	$\begin{array}{r}2\\ \times\,5\\\hline\end{array}$	$\begin{array}{r}3\\ \times\,8\\\hline\end{array}$	$\begin{array}{r}2\\ \times\,2\\\hline\end{array}$	$\begin{array}{r}9\\ \times\,8\\\hline\end{array}$
$\begin{array}{r}4\\ \times\,9\\\hline\end{array}$	$\begin{array}{r}3\\ \times\,8\\\hline\end{array}$	$\begin{array}{r}3\\ \times\,2\\\hline\end{array}$	$\begin{array}{r}3\\ \times\,9\\\hline\end{array}$	$\begin{array}{r}9\\ \times\,6\\\hline\end{array}$	$\begin{array}{r}2\\ \times\,8\\\hline\end{array}$	$\begin{array}{r}8\\ \times\,3\\\hline\end{array}$

Practice **Pretend to Add with 9**, **Rhymes**, and **Count 5,6,7,8**.

$8\times9=$ _____ $6\times8=$ _____ $7\times8=$ _____ $9\times5=$ _____

$6\times6=$ _____ $6\times9=$ _____ $9\times3=$ _____ $8\times7=$ _____

$9\times4=$ _____ $9\times7=$ _____ $8\times6=$ _____ $6\times6=$ _____

$3\times9=$ _____ $7\times8=$ _____ $9\times8=$ _____ $4\times9=$ _____

$5\times9=$ _____ $3\times9=$ _____ $6\times8=$ _____ $9\times6=$ _____

$7\times9=$ _____ $8\times9=$ _____ $8\times7=$ _____ $8\times6=$ _____

Name _____

REVIEW

Practice **Pretend to Add with 9**, **Fives**, and **I See 2 5s**.

9 × 6	8 × 5	5 × 9	5 × 5	9 × 7	9 × 4	3 × 5
3 × 9	6 × 5	7 × 5	9 × 9	5 × 7	6 × 9	5 × 4
5 × 7	7 × 9	4 × 5	9 × 8	8 × 9	7 × 5	4 × 9
5 × 5	9 × 5	3 × 5	5 × 6	5 × 5	5 × 8	9 × 3

Practice **Pretend to Add with 9**, **STRETCH**, and **Zero**.

9 × 9	5 × 9	9 × 8	6 × 0	7 × 3	0 × 7	9 × 3
0 × 1	7 × 3	6 × 9	9 × 7	4 × 0	3 × 7	9 × 5
3 × 7	3 × 0	4 × 9	3 × 7	9 × 6	0 × 8	7 × 3
3 × 9	8 × 9	7 × 3	0 × 9	3 × 7	9 × 4	7 × 9

Name _____

REVIEW
Practice **Think of 7 × 7**, **4 Fingers**, and **Rhymes**.

6 × 7	4 × 8	3 × 4	8 × 6	6 × 6	7 × 6	4 × 4
8 × 6	6 × 4	6 × 8	5 × 4	6 × 7	4 × 3	7 × 4
6 × 6	6 × 7	4 × 7	4 × 4	6 × 8	7 × 6	4 × 5
4 × 8	7 × 4	7 × 6	4 × 6	8 × 4	8 × 6	6 × 6

Practice **Think of 7 × 7**, **STRETCH**, and **Fives**.

7×6= _____	7×3= _____	5×4= _____	6×5= _____
3×7= _____	8×5= _____	3×5= _____	7×6= _____
5×6= _____	5×7= _____	6×7= _____	3×7= _____
6×7= _____	4×5= _____	7×3= _____	5×8= _____
7×5= _____	3×7= _____	7×6= _____	5×3= _____
7×3= _____	6×7= _____	8×5= _____	7×3= _____

REVIEW

Practice **Think of 7 × 7**, **I See 2 5s**, and **Fives**.

6	8	5	5	7	5	5
× 7	× 5	× 6	× 5	× 6	× 4	× 3

5	7	5	5	4	6	6
× 5	× 6	× 7	× 8	× 5	× 7	× 5

7	3	8	6	5	5	7
× 5	× 5	× 5	× 7	× 6	× 5	× 6

5	6	5	7	6	5	5
× 4	× 5	× 5	× 5	× 7	× 8	× 7

Practice **Think of 7 × 7**, **Pretend to Add**, and **Pretend to Add with 9**.

7	9	5	8	9	9	7
× 6	× 6	× 9	× 8	× 7	× 4	× 7

3	9	6	9	7	6	7
× 9	× 8	× 7	× 9	× 7	× 9	× 6

7	7	9	8	6	8	4
× 7	× 6	× 3	× 9	× 7	× 8	× 9

7	9	8	7	9	6	8
× 9	× 5	× 8	× 6	× 3	× 7	× 9

Name _____

Cumulative Practice.

7 × 6	8 × 9	5 × 4	8 × 8	9 × 3	4 × 7	8 × 6
1 × 8	7 × 3	4 × 6	8 × 5	6 × 7	3 × 3	7 × 5
6 × 9	2 × 9	5 × 5	3 × 6	9 × 8	8 × 4	6 × 0
5 × 7	6 × 6	3 × 4	9 × 9	3 × 8	7 × 3	5 × 3
7 × 8	5 × 1	4 × 4	4 × 8	6 × 5	3 × 9	9 × 5
3 × 5	9 × 7	7 × 4	4 × 3	7 × 5	6 × 8	8 × 4
0 × 4	3 × 7	9 × 8	6 × 2	5 × 9	6 × 7	9 × 3
9 × 6	4 × 5	8 × 3	4 × 9	7 × 7	5 × 8	8 × 7

Name _____

Cumulative Practice.

6 × 4	3 × 9	7 × 7	9 × 4	5 × 6	8 × 3	6 × 7
7 × 9	6 × 3	8 × 8	5 × 7	0 × 9	7 × 3	4 × 4
3 × 8	9 × 5	7 × 6	5 × 8	4 × 7	1 × 1	5 × 5
7 × 6	4 × 8	3 × 4	5 × 2	6 × 5	9 × 3	8 × 4
4 × 2	7 × 4	9 × 7	4 × 6	9 × 8	8 × 6	5 × 7
8 × 7	4 × 9	1 × 0	3 × 5	7 × 5	3 × 6	3 × 9
8 × 5	5 × 4	6 × 9	6 × 7	5 × 9	4 × 8	1 × 6
8 × 9	3 × 7	6 × 8	4 × 3	2 × 7	3 × 7	4 × 5

Five Times Five Is Not Ten: Make Multiplication Easy

Answers

Page 1
3, 8, 6
2, 5, 4, 1, 9
5, 2, 9, 3, 9, 7, 7
6, 2, 5, 8, 10, 4, 4
3, 8, 5, 8, 6, 3, 1
5, 7, 7, 2, 6, 4, 4
Page 2
7, 7
4, 4
6, 6, 9, 9, 7, 7, 1
2, 5, 4, 3, 6, 8, 4
7, 1, 7, 8, 3, 2, 9
8, 6, 4, 9, 5, 1, 3
Page 3
8, 9, 5, 7, 3, 2, 6
9, 1, 2, 6, 5, 7, 4
3, 10, 2, 4, 9, 7, 8
8, 6, 4, 5, 3, 1, 7
7, 8, 5, 4
5, 3, 6, 9
2, 3, 8, 4
7, 9, 1, 2
6, 4, 6, 7
5, 8, 1, 3
Page 4
6, 7, 7, 8
9, 2, 9, 4
6, 2, 5, 9
2, 4, 3, 6
5, 10, 8, 1
3, 8, 5, 7
3, 4, 8, 4, 3, 2, 8
6, 5, 5, 1, 3, 9, 6
1, 9, 3, 5, 4, 7, 7
2, 7, 4, 9, 8, 2, 6
Page 5
4, 4
6, 6
8, 8
10, 10
8, 10, 6, 10, 4, 8, 2
4, 6, 2, 8, 2, 10, 6
Page 6
10, 4, 1, 5, 6, 8, 3
6, 4, 10, 8, 4, 2, 6
8, 6, 2, 4, 10, 4, 10
3, 5, 4, 7, 8, 6, 9
8, 7, 4, 6
7, 2, 9, 6
6, 2, 5, 9
4, 4, 10, 8
5, 6, 1, 10
3, 8, 8, 10
Page 7
8, 8
6, 6
8, 8, 10, 6, 8, 6, 10
6, 9, 8, 5, 6, 3, 10
4, 2, 4, 10, 6, 8, 8
1, 10, 3, 6, 8, 4, 7
Page 8
10, 8, 6, 10, 4, 10, 6
4, 8, 16, 6, 10, 6, 2
6, 10, 12, 8, 8, 10, 14
10, 4, 8, 10, 6, 8, 6
6, 8, 8, 10, 6, 3, 10
4, 4, 6, 2, 10, 8, 7
10, 8, 1, 6, 2, 10, 4
8, 6, 2, 10, 5, 6, 8

Page 9
12, 12
14, 14
16, 16
18, 18
14, 18, 16, 12, 18, 14, 16
16, 14, 18, 16, 12, 18, 12
Page 10
12, 12
16, 6, 14, 18, 4, 12, 10
14, 18, 8, 16, 8, 14, 6
12, 18, 10, 14, 16, 10, 12
6, 16, 18, 8, 12, 16, 14
Page 11
18, 8, 9, 16, 14, 4, 18
8, 12, 6, 12, 6, 10, 2
16, 5, 14, 12, 16, 4, 14
3, 14, 18, 7, 18, 16, 8
16, 14, 8, 10
9, 6, 18, 2
12, 4, 7, 14
1, 8, 16, 3
4, 18, 12, 12
14, 6, 5, 16
Page 12
6, 12, 16, 6, 8, 14, 4
10, 14, 18, 16, 6, 18, 4
14, 8, 12, 10, 18, 5, 16
12, 18, 14, 3, 9, 16, 12
12, 8, 12, 6
18, 16, 14, 8
4, 10, 5, 18
6, 2, 12, 16
7, 14, 16, 6
18, 10, 18, 6
Page 13
0
0
0, 0, 0, 0, 0, 0, 0
0, 3, 0, 7, 0, 0, 5
0, 0, 9, 4, 0, 2, 0
6, 0, 8, 0, 0, 0, 1
Page 14
0, 8, 16, 0, 14, 0, 12
16, 0, 10, 0, 0, 18, 6
0, 0, 4, 8, 12, 0, 0
10, 2, 0, 18, 6, 0, 14
0, 16, 7, 0, 0, 4, 18
3, 4, 0, 14, 5, 12, 0
8, 0, 2, 10, 0, 6, 9
16, 14, 0, 12, 8, 6, 0
Page 15
0, 0
0, 0, 12, 0, 0, 16, 0
0, 10, 0, 18, 14, 0, 0
8, 0, 18, 0, 0, 6, 0
0, 0, 0, 6, 0, 4, 0
5, 2, 0, 6, 3, 0, 0
0, 0, 0, 0, 9, 0, 8
Page 16
0, 18, 0, 0
8, 0, 14, 0
0, 12, 0, 16
10, 0, 6, 0
0, 16, 0, 18
6, 0, 12, 0
0, 16, 0, 2, 12, 0, 8
18, 0, 4, 7, 5, 6, 0
9, 8, 16, 0, 0, 6, 0
4, 1, 0, 10, 3, 0, 14

Page 17
9, 8, 12, 9, 4, 6, 9
16, 10, 9, 18, 12, 9, 14
4, 9, 14, 16, 9, 18, 6
9, 18, 16, 8, 10, 9, 8
Page 18
9, 0, 0, 9, 3, 0, 5
2, 9, 4, 0, 9, 9, 9
7, 0, 9, 0, 0, 9, 8
9, 1, 0, 9, 6, 0, 0
9, 16, 6, 9
10, 9, 4, 12
8, 18, 9, 16
9, 6, 10, 9
14, 9, 8, 12
6, 18, 9, 14
Page 19
9, 9, 9, 9, 3, 9, 9
3, 9, 9, 6, 6, 9, 9
6, 9, 9, 9, 9, 3, 6
9, 9, 3, 6, 6, 9, 9
9, 0, 9, 16, 0, 9, 4
0, 3, 9, 10, 9, 0, 6
14, 9, 0, 4, 18, 6, 9
8, 8, 5, 9, 12, 9, 0
Page 20
9, 7, 6, 9, 0, 12, 5
4, 5, 8, 6, 9, 2, 14
4, 9, 0, 0, 16, 6, 1
10, 6, 6, 9, 4, 7, 9
10, 9, 4, 8
0, 7, 18, 3
9, 2, 6, 3
9, 6, 9, 6
8, 0, 3, 0
18, 5, 9, 9
Page 21
5, 6
56, 7, 56, 8, 56, 8, 56
8, 56, 7, 56, 8, 56, 7
56, 8, 56, 7, 56, 7, 56
56, 15, 56, 1, 56, 56, 0
14, 56, 56, 16, 1, 56, 15
Page 22
56, 16, 56, 9, 8, 56, 9
9, 56, 10, 56, 9, 4, 56
14, 18, 56, 9, 56, 9, 12
56, 9, 18, 56, 6, 56, 9
56, 9, 56, 6
15, 1, 9, 56
9, 56, 3, 9
1, 9, 56, 9
56, 9, 15, 56
9, 56, 9, 6
Page 23
56, 0, 56, 1, 7, 0, 56
0, 56, 8, 0, 4, 56, 9
6, 2, 0, 56, 0, 5, 56
0, 56, 3, 0, 56, 0, 0
56, 4, 10, 9, 56, 9, 16
0, 56, 6, 8, 0, 18, 56
4, 14, 56, 0, 9, 56, 8
7, 0, 6, 12, 56, 5, 56
Page 24
56, 16, 5, 15, 56, 9, 6
10, 8, 56, 7, 0, 10, 18
4, 1, 9, 8, 14, 56, 5
6, 1, 0, 56, 7, 8, 56
0, 56, 0, 12, 9, 7, 56
0, 9, 56, 2, 8, 56, 8
56, 10, 56, 9, 9, 15, 8
3, 6, 9, 0, 56, 7, 6

Page 25
25
25, 5, 25, 5, 56, 25, 7
56, 25, 8, 56, 25, 5, 56
5, 56, 7, 25, 8, 56, 25
56, 5, 25, 7, 56, 25, 56
Page 26
25, 8, 9, 12, 25, 16, 10
6, 9, 25, 14, 4, 25, 9
18, 25, 10, 6, 9, 2, 25
25, 16, 9, 25, 12, 9, 18
25, 56, 0, 25
0, 25, 56, 0
56, 0, 25, 56
25, 56, 0, 25
56, 25, 0, 0
0, 56, 25, 56
Page 27
25, 9, 6, 25, 4, 10, 5
9, 25, 4, 5, 25, 8, 6
10, 3, 8, 25, 2, 7, 25
1, 6, 25, 6, 2, 5, 3
25, 4, 18, 56, 9, 56, 0
56, 9, 12, 5, 25, 10, 25
9, 0, 25, 16, 10, 6, 56
0, 56, 8, 9, 4, 25, 14
Page 28
14, 25, 6, 5, 8, 9, 56
0, 12, 9, 25, 8, 0, 10
25, 0, 14, 56, 25, 4, 2
56, 9, 25, 2, 56, 25, 9
0, 6, 15, 25
6, 7, 10, 7
25, 0, 56, 1
1, 25, 2, 18
8, 3, 2, 0
16, 56, 25, 9
Page 29
12, 56, 12, 12, 9, 12, 56
56, 12, 56, 9, 12, 56, 12
9, 56, 12, 12, 56, 12, 9
56, 12, 9, 56, 12, 56, 12
Page 30
12, 0, 25, 12, 12, 0, 25
0, 12, 0, 25, 0, 12, 0
12, 0, 12, 0, 25, 0, 12
0, 12, 25, 12, 0, 0, 12
12, 3, 12, 16, 6, 4, 12
18, 12, 6, 12, 5, 12, 8
12, 14, 12, 1, 12, 12, 4
7, 12, 9, 8, 2, 12, 10
Page 31
12, 4, 25, 9, 12, 2, 56
56, 12, 6, 6, 12, 10
9, 12, 56, 25, 18, 9, 12
25, 12, 1, 12, 0, 56, 4
12, 3, 25, 56, 12, 0, 5
10, 12, 0, 25, 56, 9, 12
9, 56, 12, 14, 25, 16, 7
0, 12, 8, 56, 12, 0, 9
Page 32
12, 12, 5, 12, 56, 4, 25
9, 56, 12, 6, 10, 16, 12
7, 12, 10, 0, 12, 5, 0
10, 0, 12, 9, 12, 12, 56
0, 25, 2, 12, 1, 8, 18
10, 12, 9, 6, 7, 25, 7
6, 5, 8, 8, 4, 4, 12
8, 16, 12, 4, 56, 3, 14

Page 33
16, 12, 16, 12, 12, 16, 12
12, 16, 12, 8, 16, 9, 7
16, 6, 16, 12, 12, 7, 9
7, 9, 12, 16, 7, 16, 12
16, 12, 8, 6, 9, 12, 16
Page 34
12, 16, 7, 25, 9, 16, 12
8, 25, 16, 5, 12, 6, 16
12, 12, 3, 16, 2, 25, 4
16, 7, 25, 4, 16, 12, 25
16, 0, 12, 9
0, 12, 16, 0
12, 9, 0, 12
16, 0, 12, 16
9, 12, 16, 9
0, 16, 0, 12
Page 35
12, 0, 12, 16, 18, 12, 0
16, 16, 12, 10, 0, 0, 12
16, 14, 0, 12, 12, 16, 6
0, 12, 8, 0, 16, 4, 12
16, 56, 12, 25
56, 12, 25, 16
12, 25, 56, 12
12, 16, 12, 56
16, 56, 25, 12
56, 12, 16, 56
Page 36
16, 14, 12, 56, 12, 25, 8
4, 0, 16, 6, 16, 9, 0
25, 3, 0, 12, 16, 56, 12
6, 4, 56, 1, 0, 16, 9
12, 2, 18, 16, 9, 0, 12
0, 56, 12, 5, 8, 12, 16
7, 16, 25, 0, 9, 0, 56
9, 0, 56, 16, 12, 10, 25
Page 37
18, 9, 18, 18, 9, 18, 18
18, 25, 18, 9, 18, 25, 9
25, 18, 9, 18, 25, 9, 18
Page 38
18, 56, 9, 18, 56, 18, 56
9, 18, 56, 9, 18, 56, 18
56, 56, 18, 56, 9, 18, 56
18, 9, 56, 18, 18, 9, 18
18, 8, 3, 9, 18, 4, 18
9, 18, 18, 7, 1, 9, 9
9, 2, 9, 18, 6, 18, 9
18, 3, 5, 9, 18, 6, 18
Page 39
18, 9, 14, 10, 18, 8, 18
16, 18, 6, 18, 4, 18, 12
18, 12, 9, 18, 6, 14, 18
9, 8, 18, 16, 9, 18, 10
18, 16, 0, 18, 12, 18, 0
9, 18, 12, 0, 18, 9, 16
12, 0, 9, 18, 16, 18, 12
0, 12, 18, 16, 12, 0, 18
Page 40
9, 18, 9, 6
18, 9, 0, 18
3, 9, 18, 6
18, 3, 9, 18
0, 18, 6, 9
9, 18, 6, 3
18, 2, 56, 9, 12, 6, 18
16, 25, 18, 12, 8, 0, 12
9, 12, 0, 18, 56, 8, 9
10, 18, 14, 12, 16, 18, 25

Page 41
81, 9, 81, 3, 81, 5, 8
4, 81, 6, 81, 7, 81, 6
2, 7, 81, 9, 81, 4, 3
81, 1, 8, 81, 5, 2, 81
Page 42
81, 9, 18, 81, 18, 81, 9
18, 81, 9, 18, 81, 9, 18
9, 18, 81, 9, 18, 18, 81
18, 81, 18, 81, 9, 81, 18
81, 0, 0, 81
0, 25, 81, 0
25, 0, 0, 25
0, 81, 25, 0
0, 25, 0, 81
25, 0, 81, 25
Page 43
81, 10, 25, 81, 14, 4, 6
25, 16, 81, 25, 12, 18, 81
8, 81, 18, 81, 25, 81, 10
81, 25, 12, 14, 81, 16, 25
81, 56, 12, 56, 16, 81, 12
56, 12, 56, 81, 12, 56, 16
12, 56, 81, 16, 81, 12, 81
56, 81, 56, 12, 16, 56, 12
Page 44
81, 10, 56, 12, 9, 18, 9
18, 25, 0, 81, 16, 81, 56
18, 81, 5, 6, 18, 16, 81
12, 56, 81, 1, 81, 0, 18
81, 8, 18, 6, 18, 81, 4
56, 12, 25, 81, 4, 7, 12
8, 81, 0, 2, 18, 3, 12
14, 18, 81, 16, 56, 9, 0
Page 45
63, 6, 63, 8, 63, 81, 16
12, 63, 10, 63, 81, 14, 63
81, 16, 63, 18, 8, 63, 81
6, 63, 81, 63, 14, 81, 4
Page 46
63, 81, 16, 12, 63, 12, 63
12, 63, 12, 81, 12, 63, 16
81, 12, 63, 16, 63, 12, 63
16, 63, 81, 12, 16, 63, 81
63, 16, 81, 63
14, 63, 63, 18
63, 16, 18, 81
63, 81, 16, 63
16, 63, 81, 63
81, 14, 63, 81
Page 47
63, 81, 3, 56, 9, 63, 56
8, 56, 63, 7, 56, 6, 63
63, 2, 56, 63, 5, 56, 81
56, 63, 81, 4, 63, 1, 56
81, 9, 63, 18, 63, 25, 18
25, 18, 81, 63, 9, 18, 63
18, 63, 25, 81, 18, 63, 9
63, 9, 18, 63, 25, 18, 81
Page 48
63, 6, 2, 63
9, 63, 81, 0
63, 4, 63, 9
81, 0, 9, 4
3, 63, 7, 81
63, 81, 63, 8
16, 63, 6, 25, 63, 12, 10
81, 9, 56, 5, 18, 0, 63
0, 12, 63, 12, 8, 56, 81
18, 16, 18, 63, 14, 7, 63

Page 49
36, 36, 63, 36, 81, 36, 63
36, 63, 36, 81, 36, 63, 36
63, 81, 63, 36, 63, 36, 63
Page 50
36, 63, 9, 36, 18, 81, 63
18, 36, 63, 18, 9, 36, 81
63, 18, 36, 9, 63, 18, 36
81, 36, 18, 81, 36, 63, 9
63, 36, 8, 63, 81, 4, 63
81, 16, 63, 36, 14, 63, 36
18, 63, 81, 36, 6, 36, 12
36, 10, 36, 18, 63, 81, 36
Page 51
81, 56, 63, 25, 36, 56, 36
63, 25, 36, 63, 56, 36, 56
56, 36, 63, 36, 25, 56, 81
25, 63, 56, 56, 36, 63, 36
36, 81, 63, 12, 36, 16, 0
63, 12, 0, 63, 81, 0, 36
0, 63, 16, 0, 36, 12, 0
12, 0, 36, 63, 0, 36, 63
Page 52
63, 16, 18, 16, 81, 36, 12
0, 56, 25, 63, 12, 6, 9
36, 14, 4, 36, 18, 12, 63
16, 10, 18, 12, 36, 56, 0
63, 18, 12, 5, 81, 16, 8
56, 36, 25, 0, 12, 18, 4
6, 63, 12, 36, 14, 1, 16
18, 9, 56, 18, 9, 8, 63
Page 53
36, 5, 36, 12
6, 12, 7, 36
6, 36, 6, 6
36, 0, 6, 36
36, 7, 0, 36, 9, 0, 36
6, 36, 0, 0, 36, 3, 0
0, 6, 36, 8, 0, 36, 2
Page 54
36, 16, 36, 12, 36, 16, 36
12, 36, 12, 16, 12, 36, 12
36, 12, 16, 36, 12, 12, 36
16, 36, 12, 16, 36, 12, 16
36, 56, 9, 36, 18, 56, 36
18, 36, 56, 18, 36, 9, 18
56, 9, 36, 56, 18, 36, 56
18, 36, 18, 9, 56, 18, 56
Page 55
36, 63, 63, 36, 36, 63, 36
81, 36, 36, 63, 36, 36, 81
36, 81, 36, 36, 36, 63, 36
63, 36, 63, 36, 36, 36, 63
36, 25, 12, 14, 6, 36, 16
25, 8, 36, 10, 36, 4, 25
18, 36, 25, 36, 18, 25, 10
36, 16, 8, 25, 12, 14, 36
Page 56
63, 36, 12, 14, 8, 36, 56,
7, 9, 36, 36, 18, 0, 12
25, 16, 4, 63, 36, 56, 4
36, 16, 18, 5, 36, 36, 81
9, 36, 0, 36
12, 25, 6, 36
56, 18, 63, 12
36, 81, 9, 56
18, 36, 8, 18
63, 36, 16, 12
Page 57
48, 0, 25, 48, 36, 48, 0
48, 25, 36, 0, 48, 36, 25
0, 48, 0, 36, 0, 25, 48
Page 58
48, 4, 16, 48, 12, 36, 8
36, 48, 9, 12, 48, 7, 16

6, 1, 12, 48, 3, 48, 36
12, 48, 2, 36, 16, 12, 48
48, 16, 36, 12, 48, 18, 48
14, 36, 48, 6, 36, 48, 16
10, 48, 8, 48, 4, 36, 48
36, 18, 48, 14, 48, 12, 10
Page 59
36, 48, 9, 18, 9, 48, 48
18, 48, 8, 9, 48, 18, 18
48, 9, 18, 48, 18, 36, 48
18, 48, 36, 18, 48, 9, 36
48, 63, 48, 36
81, 36, 36, 48
63, 81, 63, 36
48, 36, 48, 63
36, 48, 48, 36
63, 36, 81, 48
Page 60
48, 8, 48, 12, 56, 15, 36
14, 14, 56, 48, 6, 48, 56
36, 7, 48, 15, 56, 36, 48
56, 48, 16, 56, 8, 48, 14
48, 3, 25, 16, 12, 48, 36
63, 9, 48, 18, 10, 16, 0
18, 14, 63, 0, 56, 5, 6
36, 16, 12, 81, 48, 12, 56
Page 61
15
15, 36, 48, 15, 15, 48, 36
48, 15, 36, 15, 48, 15, 48
36, 48, 15, 48, 15, 36, 15
15, 36, 48, 15, 48, 15, 48
Page 62
15, 14, 8, 15, 15, 16, 18
4, 15, 12, 15, 8, 15, 6
10, 18, 15, 12, 15, 14, 15
15, 6, 16, 15, 10, 15, 4
15, 2, 56, 4, 15, 56, 8
1, 15, 7, 56, 5, 15, 9
56, 3, 15, 8, 15, 6, 56
15, 56, 5, 15, 9, 56, 4
Page 63
15, 15, 12, 0, 15, 12, 0
12, 15, 0, 16, 0, 15, 12
15, 0, 15, 0, 12, 16, 15
0, 12, 16, 15, 0, 0, 12
15, 63, 15, 25
36, 81, 25, 15
15, 36, 15, 63
25, 15, 36, 15
63, 36, 15, 81
36, 15, 63, 15
Page 64
15, 9, 18, 18, 15, 15, 9
18, 15, 18, 15, 9, 18, 15
9, 15, 9, 18, 15, 18, 15
15, 18, 15, 9, 18, 15, 18
15, 9, 18, 15
6, 18, 15, 2
18, 8, 9, 18
3, 15, 1, 0
15, 5, 18, 8
9, 15, 9, 18
Page 65
4, 15, 36, 48, 4, 15, 63
12, 56, 6, 25, 16, 0, 15
0, 18, 36, 36, 15, 56, 81
48, 63, 9, 16, 12, 5, 18
12, 15, 56, 0, 18, 18, 16
63, 36, 8, 15, 36, 36, 25
14, 18, 0, 48, 9, 81, 15
15, 48, 12, 3, 56, 15, 63
Page 66
48, 8, 15, 36, 15, 12, 81
1, 18, 0, 12, 63, 48, 36

9, 25, 56, 15, 16, 36, 15
63, 8, 12, 56, 48, 15, 0
36, 15, 36, 63, 12, 2, 10
18, 6, 25, 81, 0, 15, 56
18, 16, 48, 15, 56, 36, 12
15, 8, 18, 63, 15, 0, 18
Page 67
54, 54, 81, 63, 54, 36, 54
63, 81, 54, 36, 63, 54, 36
36, 54, 63, 54, 36, 81, 63
Page 68
54, 9, 36, 54, 4, 54, 81
7, 54, 63, 3, 63, 36, 54
63, 81, 54, 36, 2, 6, 36
36, 8, 5, 63, 54, 63, 54
63, 54, 48, 36, 54, 48, 36
54, 48, 63, 48, 36, 54, 81
48, 36, 54, 36, 36, 63, 54
54, 48, 36, 54, 48, 36, 63
Page 69
36, 54, 15, 54, 15, 63, 15
54, 15, 81, 36, 54, 15, 63
15, 63, 54, 15, 63, 36, 54
63, 54, 15, 81, 36, 54, 81
54, 36, 63, 12, 16, 54, 12
36, 54, 12, 54, 36, 15, 54
81, 63, 16, 12, 54, 36, 63
54, 12, 36, 63, 36, 12, 54
Page 70
54, 56, 36, 18
63, 9, 54, 56
18, 36, 56, 54
56, 63, 54, 36
9, 54, 18, 56
54, 18, 36, 63
63, 16, 9, 54, 0, 36, 15
4, 48, 8, 36, 18, 81, 54
14, 15, 56, 12, 54, 8, 48
36, 18, 25, 54, 63, 56, 12
Page 71
45, 63, 45, 0, 54, 45, 36
54, 45, 0, 81, 0, 54, 0
36, 0, 63, 45, 54, 0, 45
Page 72
63, 45, 8, 54, 45, 6, 48
36, 9, 36, 45, 48, 81, 45
7, 48, 45, 36, 63, 45, 3
45, 36, 48, 1, 45, 5, 54
54, 9, 45, 63
45, 36, 81, 45
18, 63, 54, 18
36, 45, 18, 54
81, 9, 45, 36
63, 45, 18, 45
Page 73
45, 12, 63, 45, 54, 25, 16
12, 54, 45, 36, 45, 12, 63
25, 36, 16, 12, 54, 45, 36
45, 63, 12, 45, 25, 54, 45
45, 16, 36, 54
63, 45, 14, 10
54, 18, 54, 45
12, 81, 45, 63
36, 6, 63, 54
45, 8, 45, 36
Page 74
36, 15, 45, 15, 54, 45, 15
54, 45, 15, 63, 56, 36, 45
15, 63, 54, 56, 45, 15, 54
45, 15, 36, 15, 63, 56, 15
81, 16, 45, 54, 18, 13, 63
36, 54, 14, 15, 36, 14, 45
15, 81, 54, 45, 16, 36, 54
45, 13, 16, 18, 25, 63, 14

Page 75
24, 14, 24, 18, 24, 6, 24
8, 24, 10, 16, 6, 24, 12
24, 6, 24, 24, 16, 18, 24
Page 76
24, 8, 12, 24, 4, 12, 24
12, 24, 3, 12, 16, 24, 12
4, 16, 24, 24, 8, 12, 24
24, 1, 12, 16, 24, 3, 12
24, 11, 24, 16
3, 24, 0, 24
24, 3, 24, 7
9, 2, 11, 8
6, 24, 0, 24
24, 8, 24, 4
Page 77
24, 63, 45, 24, 54, 24, 36
81, 24, 24, 63, 24, 36, 63
24, 45, 36, 54, 45, 54, 24
54, 36, 81, 24, 63, 24, 45
24, 56, 24, 9, 18, 18, 56
18, 24, 18, 56, 24, 56, 9
56, 18, 56, 24, 9, 18, 24
24, 56, 24, 18, 56, 24, 18
Page 78
24, 48, 36, 0, 24, 24, 0
36, 24, 48, 24, 0, 0, 24
48, 0, 24, 48, 24, 48, 36
24, 36, 0, 24, 48, 0, 24
24, 15, 24, 24, 25, 24, 15
15, 24, 25, 15, 24, 15, 24
25, 15, 24, 24, 15, 25, 15
24, 24, 15, 24, 15, 25, 25
Page 79
24, 45, 7, 8, 16, 54, 36
63, 15, 24, 15, 48, 0, 24
6, 24, 56, 45, 24, 10, 12
48, 0, 18, 24, 36, 9, 54
16, 54, 24, 25, 45, 24, 0
24, 12, 48, 2, 56, 18, 24
15, 63, 54, 24, 36, 15, 48
4, 24, 5, 0, 18, 81, 45
Page 80
16, 24, 15, 36, 16, 45, 24
0, 63, 54, 9, 24, 18, 8
24, 25, 36, 56, 0, 54, 81
18, 2, 24, 12, 48, 9, 63
4, 56, 6, 36
24, 45, 63, 3
15, 4, 18, 24
45, 12, 16, 12
48, 1, 0, 56
10, 24, 36, 54
Page 81
20, 16, 20, 20, 24, 20, 12
12, 20, 16, 20, 24, 12, 20
20, 24, 12, 20, 16, 24, 12
24, 20, 24, 16, 12, 20, 24
Page 82
20, 12, 56, 20, 16, 12, 20
56, 16, 20, 56, 12, 20, 56
20, 56, 16, 20, 56, 20, 16
12, 20, 56, 12, 20, 56, 20
12, 63, 20, 16, 54, 20, 45
36, 20, 12, 63, 20, 54, 16
20, 12, 45, 20, 12, 81, 20
45, 16, 12, 54, 36, 20, 12
Page 83
20, 15, 16, 20, 25, 12, 15
15, 20, 12, 25, 20, 15, 20
25, 16, 20, 12, 15, 25, 12
20, 15, 12, 20, 12, 15, 16
20, 48, 16, 36
12, 20, 48, 12
36, 12, 20, 20

48, 20, 12, 48
20, 16, 20, 12
48, 36, 12, 20
Page 84
20, 16, 18, 16, 14, 12, 20
9, 12, 18, 20, 18, 20, 10
18, 6, 12, 12, 9, 4, 18
12, 20, 18, 16, 8, 18, 20
16, 4, 0, 8, 0, 20, 1
0, 20, 7, 12, 9, 0, 20
0, 12, 3, 20, 5, 20, 0
12, 6, 20, 0, 9, 12, 16
Page 85
24, 16, 24, 3, 24, 20, 12
6, 24, 8, 20, 0, 2, 24, 4
12, 20, 24, 5, 12, 7, 16
24, 9, 20, 24, 1, 12, 24
Page 86
24, 12, 10, 24, 8, 24, 20
16, 20, 24, 14, 16, 12, 24
8, 6, 16, 20, 24, 18, 12
20, 24, 4, 12, 12, 24, 16
12, 24, 15, 24
15, 20, 16, 20
24, 24, 20, 15
24, 20, 15, 12
16, 15, 20, 24
12, 24, 15, 12
Page 87
16, 36, 24, 20, 12, 48, 24
48, 24, 20, 36, 20, 24, 48
24, 16, 48, 12, 24, 36, 12
36, 48, 24, 20, 48, 12, 24
24, 25, 0, 12, 25, 20, 24
0, 12, 24, 20, 12, 0, 20
16, 24, 0, 0, 24, 16, 0
20, 0, 25, 24, 0, 20, 12
Page 88
12, 24, 56, 16, 12, 56, 24
24, 24, 20, 56, 20, 24, 24
24, 56, 16, 12, 24, 24, 12
56, 20, 24, 24, 56, 20, 24
20, 45, 24, 12, 24, 16, 81
63, 24, 20, 45, 54, 24, 12
36, 12, 54, 63, 36, 63, 24
16, 45, 24, 54, 20, 36, 54
Page 89
28, 0, 24, 56, 0, 28, 16
56, 28, 20, 28, 12, 0, 56
24, 56, 28, 0, 56, 20, 28
0, 28, 56, 24, 28, 0, 12
Page 90
28, 14, 28, 12, 7, 20, 28
8, 24, 16, 28, 20, 7, 6
20, 28, 0, 24, 28, 12, 9
24, 0, 28, 16, 24, 28, 12
24, 28, 4, 12, 28, 25, 20
28, 6, 12, 25, 24, 7, 28
16, 25, 28, 7, 12, 28, 4
5, 20, 6, 28, 20, 24, 25
Page 91
12, 45, 36, 24, 28, 24, 28
63, 24, 28, 54, 20, 45, 24
28, 54, 24, 28, 24, 16, 24
81, 36, 20, 12, 28, 63, 24
28, 48, 24, 48, 20, 28, 15
36, 15, 12, 28, 48, 16, 28
15, 28, 48, 12, 15, 24, 36
28, 48, 15, 36, 28, 20, 48
Page 92
20, 18, 28, 15, 63, 36, 12
10, 18, 0, 28, 48, 3, 24
45, 48, 9, 56, 24, 54, 16
24, 28, 15, 6, 20, 14, 36
18, 56, 24, 0

16, 25, 36, 24
12, 28, 2, 15
24, 81, 56, 36
28, 48, 12, 63
45, 18, 28, 54
Page 93
49, 6, 49, 14
7, 0, 8, 49
7, 49, 7, 7
49, 0, 49, 8
49, 56, 49, 56, 56, 49, 56
56, 49, 56, 49, 56, 56, 49
Page 94
49, 24, 28, 49, 12, 49, 20
28, 16, 49, 20, 49, 28, 12
20, 49, 24, 49, 28, 12, 49
24, 28, 49, 12, 20, 49, 24
49, 54, 36, 49, 45, 36, 49
54, 45, 49, 81, 54, 49, 63
81, 49, 63, 36, 49, 45, 36
49, 63, 54, 63, 45, 49, 81
Page 95
49, 2, 18, 9, 8, 49, 5
18, 7, 49, 18, 3, 9, 49
3, 49, 9, 4, 49, 18, 9
9, 18, 6, 49, 18, 7, 9
49, 36, 8, 48
10, 14, 48, 49
16, 48, 49, 18
36, 49, 6, 48
4, 12, 48, 49
14, 36, 49, 48
Page 96
49, 24, 24, 49, 15, 24, 15
24, 49, 15, 24, 49, 15, 49
24, 15, 49, 15, 24, 49, 15
15, 49, 15, 24, 15, 24, 49
9, 49, 45, 24
24, 25, 36, 36
9, 12, 0, 48
49, 63, 18, 8
20, 12, 54, 28
56, 28, 49, 15
Page 97
64, 7, 64, 49
0, 64, 9, 6
49, 0, 49, 64
16, 49, 64, 14
64, 49, 64, 24, 49, 24, 49
24, 64, 24, 64, 24, 49, 64
Page 98
64, 36, 64, 49, 45, 64, 63
49, 25, 54, 81, 64, 36, 49
45, 49, 64, 63, 25, 45, 64
54, 63, 25, 64, 54, 64, 36
49, 6, 64, 14, 56, 10, 64
16, 64, 49, 56, 18, 64, 56
64, 49, 8, 64, 56, 49, 12
4, 56, 64, 56, 14, 64, 16
Page 99
49, 0, 18, 64, 49, 18, 0
64, 18, 64, 9, 18, 0, 64
0, 64, 0, 18, 0, 64, 49
18, 0, 49, 0, 64, 9, 0
64, 48, 28, 64
20, 36, 48, 24
49, 28, 16, 49
48, 49, 64, 12
36, 24, 36, 48
12, 64, 49, 20
Page 100
16, 63, 12, 64, 28, 18, 0
28, 15, 49, 36, 48, 16, 45
64, 1, 20, 56, 24, 24, 12
81, 54, 64, 24, 6, 0, 64

49, 48, 15, 64, 45, 8, 56
24, 6, 36, 0, 9, 28, 64
63, 9, 49, 12, 10, 25, 20
14, 64, 36, 28, 54, 18, 18
Page 101
30, 40, 20, 40, 30, 15, 20
40, 20, 15, 30, 40, 20, 30
15, 30, 20, 40, 30, 15, 40
40, 20, 30, 15, 40, 30, 15
Page 102
30, 40, 20, 30, 25, 40, 15
25, 30, 15, 40, 40, 20, 30
40, 15, 25, 15, 20, 30, 25
30, 20, 30, 40, 15, 25, 40
40, 20, 0, 30, 0, 15, 0
0, 30, 40, 0, 40, 30, 20
30, 15, 0, 40, 0, 20, 15
20, 40, 15, 30, 40, 0, 30
Page 103
40, 64, 30, 20, 15, 49, 40
20, 30, 49, 40, 64, 20, 15
30, 15, 64, 30, 49, 40, 64
49, 40, 20, 15, 40, 30, 30
30, 40, 15, 16
4, 20, 12, 30
40, 18, 16, 14
15, 30, 4, 8
10, 40, 20, 18
30, 6, 40, 15
Page 104
20, 40, 30, 24, 30, 15, 24
15, 24, 40, 15, 24, 20, 30
24, 40, 30, 40, 20, 30, 40
30, 24, 24, 40, 40, 24, 15
40, 30, 16, 12, 40, 28, 24
15, 20, 40, 20, 30, 24, 28
30, 12, 15, 28, 12, 40, 20
16, 28, 24, 40, 24, 12, 30
Page 105
20, 25, 48, 40, 15, 48, 30
40, 48, 36, 20, 25, 30, 15
30, 36, 25, 15, 48, 40, 20
48, 15, 20, 48, 30, 36, 40
40, 30, 64, 18, 49, 20, 18
15, 40, 49, 30, 18, 64, 9
20, 15, 30, 40, 15, 49, 30
64, 18, 15, 9, 20, 40, 20
Page 106
40, 28, 16, 56, 30, 12, 15
12, 30, 56, 15, 20, 56, 24
28, 16, 15, 24, 56, 40, 16
20, 24, 30, 40, 28, 20, 56
15, 16, 6, 30
49, 12, 64, 18
40, 30, 8, 20
64, 49, 40, 14
10, 20, 15, 49
30, 4, 40, 64
Page 107
64, 7, 48, 6, 36, 49, 48
9, 49, 3, 64, 5, 48, 8
36, 4, 49, 48, 2, 64, 1
48, 5, 64, 7, 48, 36, 49
49, 24, 18, 12, 24, 8, 64
24, 14, 16, 64, 49, 24, 10
12, 64, 24, 10, 24, 4, 49
14, 24, 49, 24, 8, 64, 6
Page 108
12, 28, 24, 63, 45, 81, 16
28, 63, 36, 12, 54, 20, 45
54, 16, 20, 36, 12, 63, 24
24, 45, 28, 24, 20, 36, 54
20, 12, 25, 28
64, 49, 24, 16
28, 20, 12, 49

24, 64, 16, 25
49, 25, 20, 28
12, 24, 64, 20
Page 109
24, 25, 18, 18, 24, 9, 24
9, 18, 24, 25, 24, 18, 25
24, 9, 18, 24, 18, 25, 9
18, 24, 9, 18, 25, 24, 18
24, 63, 56, 36, 45, 56, 24
45, 56, 81, 54, 24, 54, 56
63, 24, 56, 45, 56, 24, 36
54, 36, 24, 56, 81, 45, 63
Page 110
54, 45, 40, 30, 63, 36, 15
36, 30, 81, 15, 40, 54, 20
40, 63, 20, 45, 54, 30, 36
45, 20, 15, 30, 15, 40, 63
63, 48, 9, 36
18, 54, 45, 18
36, 81, 36, 48
48, 9, 63, 36
45, 36, 48, 54
18, 48, 18, 48
Page 111
35, 20, 35, 15, 35, 30, 35
40, 35, 15, 30, 20, 35, 15
15, 30, 35, 40, 15, 20, 35
40, 15, 30, 35, 40, 35, 20
Page 112
35, 30, 35, 18, 40, 35, 20
18, 35, 40, 15, 18, 20, 35
15, 9, 18, 35, 30, 35, 40
35, 20, 35, 30, 35, 9, 15
35, 18, 30, 35, 56, 6, 35
20, 35, 56, 12, 35, 56, 14
40, 16, 35, 20, 15, 35, 10
56, 15, 8, 40, 30, 56, 35
Page 113
40, 35, 4, 64, 35, 15, 3
35, 6, 30, 20, 49, 2, 35
7, 64, 35, 8, 1, 35, 30
49, 35, 5, 40, 20, 9, 15
35, 48, 20, 40
24, 35, 36, 30
40, 15, 24, 35
35, 36, 48, 15
24, 35, 30, 35
48, 20, 24, 48
Page 114
54, 35, 16, 35, 0, 48, 15
25, 24, 56, 12, 49, 20, 35
36, 81, 12, 64, 35, 7, 24
28, 4, 35, 18, 16, 40, 63
35, 36, 15, 7
45, 20, 6, 35
0, 56, 28, 48
54, 30, 24, 45
10, 5, 63, 40
18, 24, 35, 30
Page 115
32, 32, 16, 14, 32, 24, 32
20, 8, 32, 12, 28, 32, 18
32, 24, 10, 6, 16, 12, 32
4, 20, 32, 28, 16, 32, 12
Page 116
32, 8, 32, 16, 4, 24, 32
0, 32, 12, 32, 28, 12, 1
20, 10, 32, 1, 32, 12, 32
28, 32, 12, 20, 16, 32, 24
28, 32, 24, 32, 49, 16, 32
32, 12, 20, 24, 64, 32, 24
49, 28, 32, 12, 16, 20, 64
32, 24, 64, 20, 32, 49, 28
Page 117
16, 32, 28, 18, 32, 20, 9

18, 24, 32, 28, 12, 25, 32
28, 32, 25, 24, 18, 32, 12
32, 9, 20, 32, 25, 24, 18
32, 45, 28, 54, 32, 63, 24
63, 32, 12, 16, 54, 32, 20
28, 81, 36, 20, 32, 12, 32
20, 63, 32, 24, 45, 32, 36
Page 118
32, 28, 30, 20, 12, 35, 32
15, 40, 35, 24, 30, 32, 16
40, 32, 12, 28, 32, 15, 40
32, 35, 20, 40, 24, 35, 30
28, 20, 24, 24, 24, 28, 32
24, 12, 32, 20, 32, 24, 24
16, 24, 12, 24, 32, 12, 28
24, 32, 24, 32, 20, 24, 24
Page 119
21, 28, 32, 21, 21, 16, 21
24, 32, 21, 20, 28, 21, 32
21, 12, 32, 21, 24, 28, 21
20, 21, 16, 32, 21, 12, 32
Page 120
21, 25, 21, 30, 40, 21, 15
30, 21, 20, 21, 35, 25, 21
21, 40, 15, 21, 21, 35, 20
25, 15, 30, 35, 25, 21, 40
21, 63, 54, 21, 7, 21, 45
3, 21, 1, 36, 21, 8, 9
81, 7, 21, 45, 63, 21, 5
21, 36, 6, 21, 3, 54, 21
Page 121
21, 24, 48, 21, 48, 36, 21
24, 36, 21, 48, 24, 21, 24
48, 21, 24, 24, 21, 48, 36
24, 48, 21, 21, 48, 21, 24
21, 56, 21, 9, 18, 21, 56
18, 21, 56, 18, 21, 9, 21
56, 56, 21, 9, 18, 56, 18
18, 21, 56, 21, 56, 21, 9
Page 122
21, 10, 0, 21, 0, 21, 0
0, 7, 3, 0, 21, 3, 21
7, 0, 21, 0, 3, 21, 7
21, 0, 0, 10, 0, 0, 0
21, 6, 21, 64
18, 21, 49, 8
49, 14, 10, 21
12, 64, 21, 6
21, 49, 14, 16
64, 21, 64, 21
Page 123
25, 21, 24, 6, 21, 40, 36
32, 48, 21, 36, 5, 24, 21
49, 0, 63, 21, 45, 28, 54
24, 45, 16, 15, 64, 56, 12
32, 4, 48, 35
63, 30, 9, 0
21, 20, 81, 28
40, 16, 21, 36
24, 35, 18, 30
4, 21, 54, 56
Page 124
48, 36, 12, 14, 32, 64, 21
15, 24, 0, 45, 35, 24, 36
21, 28, 20, 63, 18, 49, 15
54, 9, 21, 16, 30, 9, 56
21, 81, 32, 35, 0, 21, 18
25, 40, 20, 21, 28, 12, 36
56, 24, 24, 12, 45, 30, 54
8, 21, 18, 48, 63, 21, 40
Page 125
42, 49, 42, 64
49, 42, 49, 42
42, 64, 42, 49
64, 42, 64, 42

Page 126
42, 49, 42, 21, 42, 49, 21
64, 42, 21, 49, 64, 42, 49
42, 21, 42, 21, 42, 64, 42
21, 64, 49, 42, 21, 21, 64
42, 30, 49, 42, 64, 20, 42
40, 42, 15, 49, 42, 42, 64
49, 35, 42, 30, 40, 35, 42
15, 42, 64, 40, 42, 35, 20
Page 127
42, 32, 24, 42, 12, 42, 24
20, 42, 32, 16, 42, 20, 12
28, 16, 42, 20, 32, 42, 28
12, 42, 28, 42, 24, 32, 42
42, 63, 36, 42, 24, 54, 45
24, 36, 42, 45, 54, 42, 24
81, 42, 63, 24, 42, 36, 42
54, 24, 45, 42, 81, 24, 63
Page 128
42, 48, 36, 25, 42, 48, 48
25, 42, 48, 42, 48, 36, 42
48, 36, 42, 48, 25, 42, 36
42, 48, 25, 36, 42, 48, 42
42, 16, 18, 42
6, 42, 9, 14
18, 42, 10, 9
42, 18, 42, 18
18, 8, 18, 42
12, 9, 42, 18
Page 129
72, 72, 27, 27, 45, 72, 27
63, 27, 72, 36, 27, 54, 72
Page 130
72, 9, 27, 18, 27, 54, 72
63, 27, 72, 27, 81, 36, 18
18, 45, 27, 72, 18, 9, 72
27, 72, 54, 18, 72, 18, 27
72, 16, 27, 72
45, 27, 13, 63
17, 72, 12, 27
81, 14, 72, 45
27, 36, 15, 17
12, 54, 27, 72
Page 131
27, 72, 42, 42, 45, 72
42, 27, 42, 72, 36, 42, 27
36, 42, 63, 27, 42, 72, 54
42, 72, 27, 45, 63, 27, 72
72, 56, 72, 54
27, 72, 27, 56
45, 56, 36, 27
56, 72, 81, 27
36, 27, 56, 72
27, 63, 72, 56
Page 132
27, 72, 21, 45, 27, 54, 21
36, 21, 81, 72, 63, 21, 27
72, 54, 27, 36, 21, 45, 72
21, 27, 72, 21, 72, 27, 21
72, 27, 45, 24, 63, 72, 27
54, 27, 24, 81, 72, 36, 24
72, 24, 36, 72, 27, 27, 63
24, 63, 72, 27, 45, 54, 24
Page 133
42, 9, 42, 0, 18, 42, 0
18, 0, 0, 9, 42, 0, 18
0, 18, 0, 42, 0, 18, 42
9, 42, 18, 0, 0, 42, 18
42, 64, 49, 42
25, 42, 42, 64
49, 25, 64, 42
64, 42, 42, 49
42, 25, 49, 42
64, 42, 42, 25

Page 134
42, 42, 48, 36, 56, 48, 56
36, 48, 42, 56, 42, 56, 42
56, 42, 56, 36, 48, 42, 48
48, 36, 42, 48, 56, 48, 56
42, 24, 28, 12
42, 20, 24, 32
16, 42, 24, 20
24, 32, 12, 42
24, 28, 32, 28
42, 24, 42, 24
Page 135
42, 21, 7, 42, 21, 3, 21
42, 1, 21, 8, 21, 7, 42
2, 21, 42, 21, 9, 42, 21
42, 4, 21, 5, 42, 21, 6
42, 21, 18, 21
16, 10, 42, 12
4, 21, 8, 14
21, 16, 42, 21
42, 21, 6, 42
18, 42, 14, 12
Page 136
42, 72, 21, 21, 42, 36, 42
21, 45, 42, 27, 54, 21, 72
27, 21, 45, 72, 27, 42, 81
72, 42, 27, 36, 42, 54, 21
42, 21, 24, 42, 24, 42, 21
24, 24, 42, 21, 42, 24, 42
21, 42, 24, 42, 24, 21, 21
42, 24, 21, 24, 42, 21, 24
Page 137
15, 24, 0, 35, 30, 0, 35
0, 40, 24, 15, 35, 24, 0
24, 35, 20, 0, 15, 30, 24
0, 20, 35, 35, 24, 0, 40
35, 15, 42, 30
49, 30, 64, 42
40, 35, 40, 20
64, 49, 35, 42
20, 42, 15, 49
30, 15, 35, 64
Page 138
35, 30, 48, 40, 15, 36, 35
40, 48, 20, 48, 36, 20, 15
30, 36, 35, 36, 48, 40, 20
48, 20, 15, 35, 30, 35, 40
15, 21, 18, 18, 40, 21, 9
20, 18, 21, 35, 21, 35, 40
21, 30, 9, 18, 15, 21, 20
18, 21, 35, 21, 35, 30, 18
Page 139
21, 9, 36, 48, 21, 7, 8
48, 36, 21, 2, 48, 21, 48
5, 48, 4, 21, 36, 48, 21
36, 21, 21, 48, 6, 48, 3
21, 25, 21, 64
49, 64, 25, 21
64, 21, 64, 49
21, 49, 21, 21
25, 64, 21, 25
49, 21, 25, 49
Page 140
21, 25, 56, 21, 25, 56, 56
25, 56, 21, 56, 21, 25, 21
56, 21, 25, 21, 56, 21, 56
21, 56, 21, 25, 21, 56, 25
21, 9, 18, 24
24, 18, 21, 9
21, 24, 21, 24
18, 21, 18, 21
24, 9, 21, 18
9, 21, 18, 24
Page 141
32, 49, 42, 24, 42, 24, 20

64, 42, 49, 28, 32, 12, 42
12, 32, 64, 42, 49, 16, 64
20, 24, 28, 32, 42, 49, 28
28, 40, 16, 56, 24, 12, 15
32, 30, 28, 35, 20, 56, 32
24, 56, 15, 24, 56, 40, 12
35, 32, 30, 56, 32, 20, 28
Page 142
32, 81, 24, 72, 45, 12, 16
28, 63, 36, 27, 54, 20, 45
72, 16, 20, 36, 63, 27, 24
12, 72, 28, 32, 27, 28, 54
16, 42, 42, 24, 21, 32, 21
42, 12, 21, 28, 42, 12, 28
21, 32, 24, 21, 20, 42, 24
28, 21, 42, 16, 12, 21, 32
Page 143
63, 24, 18, 12, 24, 8, 36
16, 72, 14, 54, 27, 24, 45
45, 12, 63, 10, 24, 4, 72
36, 24, 6, 27, 54, 16, 24
72, 48, 56, 45
36, 54, 27, 56
36, 63, 48, 36
27, 56, 72, 36
45, 27, 48, 54
63, 72, 56, 48
Page 144
54, 40, 45, 25, 63, 36, 15
27, 30, 35, 81, 35, 54, 20
35, 63, 20, 72, 72, 35, 36
25, 45, 15, 30, 25, 40, 27
81, 45, 72, 0, 21, 0, 27
0, 21, 54, 63, 0, 21, 45
21, 0, 36, 21, 54, 0, 21
27, 72, 21, 0, 21, 36, 63
Page 145
42, 32, 12, 48, 36, 42, 16
48, 24, 48, 20, 42, 12, 28
36, 42, 28, 16, 48, 42, 20
32, 28, 42, 24, 32, 48, 36
42, 21, 20, 30
21, 40, 15, 42
30, 35, 42, 21
42, 20, 21, 40
35, 21, 42, 15
21, 42, 40, 21
Page 146
42, 40, 30, 25, 42, 20, 15
25, 42, 35, 40, 20, 42, 30
35, 15, 40, 42, 30, 25, 42
20, 30, 35, 25, 42, 40, 35
42, 54, 45, 64, 63, 36, 49
27, 72, 42, 81, 49, 54, 42
49, 42, 27, 72, 42, 64, 36
63, 45, 64, 42, 27, 42, 72
Page 147
42, 72, 20, 64, 27, 28, 48
8, 21, 24, 40, 42, 9, 35
54, 18, 25, 18, 72, 32, 0
35, 36, 12, 81, 24, 21, 15
56, 5, 16, 32, 30, 27, 45
15, 63, 28, 12, 35, 48, 32
0, 21, 72, 12, 45, 42, 27
54, 20, 24, 36, 49, 40, 56
Page 148
24, 27, 49, 36, 30, 24, 42
63, 18, 64, 35, 0, 21, 16
24, 45, 42, 40, 28, 1, 25
42, 32, 12, 30, 27, 32
8, 28, 63, 24, 72, 48, 35
56, 36, 0, 15, 35, 18, 27
40, 20, 54, 42, 45, 32, 6
72, 21, 48, 12, 14, 21, 20

Congratulations

to _____

date _____

for Mastery
of Multiplication
Math Facts

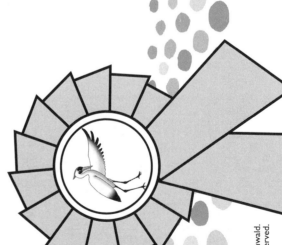

Math Facts Baseline Recorder

Multiplication

Name _____

Baseline Date _____   Multiplication Facts: + _____ / 81

Circle KNOWN facts.   Check KNOWN concepts of Zero.

81 Multiplication Facts

Concepts of Zero: (Number × Zero) _____   (Zero × Number) _____

1 × 1,	1 × 2,	1 × 3,	1 × 4,	1 × 5,	1 × 6,	1 × 7,	1 × 8,	1 × 9,
2 × 1,	2 × 2,	2 × 3,	2 × 4,	2 × 5,	2 × 6,	2 × 7,	2 × 8,	2 × 9,
3 × 1,	3 × 2,	3 × 3,	3 × 4,	3 × 5,	3 × 6,	3 × 7,	3 × 8,	3 × 9,
4 × 1,	4 × 2,	4 × 3,	4 × 4,	4 × 5,	4 × 6,	4 × 7,	4 × 8,	4 × 9,
5 × 1,	5 × 2,	5 × 3,	5 × 4,	5 × 5,	5 × 6,	5 × 7,	5 × 8,	5 × 9,
6 × 1,	6 × 2,	6 × 3,	6 × 4,	6 × 5,	6 × 6,	6 × 7,	6 × 8,	6 × 9,
7 × 1,	7 × 2,	7 × 3,	7 × 4,	7 × 5,	7 × 6,	7 × 7,	7 × 8,	7 × 9,
8 × 1,	8 × 2,	8 × 3,	8 × 4,	8 × 5,	8 × 6,	8 × 7,	8 × 8,	8 × 9,
9 × 1,	9 × 2,	9 × 3,	9 × 4,	9 × 5,	9 × 6,	9 × 7,	9 × 8,	9 × 9,

Record-Keeping Checklist

Notes	Workbook Page	Facts in Order of Introduction
_____	Page 1	1×1 1×2 1×3 1×4 1×5 1×6 1×7 1×8 1×9
		2×1 3×1 4×1 5×1 6×1 7×1 8×1 9×1
_____	Page 5	2×2 2×3 2×4 2×5 3×2 4×2 5×2
_____	Page 9	2×6 2×7 2×8 2×9 6×2 7×2 8×2 9×2
_____	Page 13	1×0 2×0 3×0 4×0 5×0 6×0 7×0 8×0 9×0
		0×1 0×2 0×3 0×4 0×5 0×6 0×7 0×8 0×9 0×0
_____	Page 17	3×3
_____	Page 21	7×8 8×7
_____	Page 25	5×5
_____	Page 29	4×3 3×4
_____	Page 33	4×4
_____	Page 37	3×6 6×3
_____	Page 41	9×9
_____	Page 45	7×9 9×7
_____	Page 49	4×9 9×4
_____	Page 53	6×6
_____	Page 57	6×8 8×6
_____	Page 61	5×3 3×5
_____	Page 67	6×9 9×6
_____	Page 71	5×9 9×5
_____	Page 75	3×8 8×3
_____	Page 81	4×5 5×4
_____	Page 85	4×6 6×4
_____	Page 89	4×7 7×4
_____	Page 93	7×7
_____	Page 97	8×8
_____	Page 101	5×6 6×5 5×8 8×5
_____	Page 111	5×7 7×5
_____	Page 115	4×8 8×4
_____	Page 119	3×7 7×3
_____	Page 125	6×7 7×6
_____	Page 129	8×9 9×8 3×9 9×3

Name _____   Baseline Date _____

Index of Facts by Name

1 Group, 1-4, 6-7, 11, 13, 18, 21, 23, 25, 27, 30, 34, 38, 41, 47, 53, 58, 62, 68, 72, 76, 85, 90, 95, 107, 113, 120, 135, 139

4 Fingers, 29-30, 33-35, 39, 43, 46, 51, 54, 58, 63, 69, 73, 76, 81-91, 94, 99, 104, 106, 108, 115-119, 127, 134, 141-142, 145

Count by 3s, 17-19, 22, 26, 29, 33-34, 37-40, 42, 47, 50, 54, 59, 64, 70, 72, 77, 84, 95, 99, 105, 109-110, 112, 117, 121, 128, 130, 133, 138, 140

Count 5,6,7,8, 21-23, 25-26, 29, 35, 38, 43, 47, 51, 54, 60, 62, 70, 74, 77, 82, 88-89, 93, 98, 106, 109, 112, 121, 131, 134, 140-141, 143

Doubles, 5-12, 14-18, 22, 26, 30, 35, 39, 43, 45, 50, 55, 58, 62, 73, 75, 84, 86, 95, 98, 103, 106-107, 112, 115, 122, 128, 135, 143

Fives, 61-64, 69, 74, 78, 83, 86, 91, 96, 101-106, 110-113, 118, 120, 126, 137-138, 141, 144-146

I See 2 5s, 25-27, 30, 34-35, 37, 42-43, 47, 51, 55, 57, 63, 73, 78, 83, 87, 90, 98, 102, 105, 108-109, 117, 120, 128, 133, 139-140, 144, 146

Pretend to Add, 93-99, 103, 105-108, 113, 116, 122, 125-126, 133, 137, 139, 141, 146

Pretend to Add with 9, 41-43, 45-51, 55, 59, 63, 67-74, 77, 82, 88, 91, 94, 98, 108-110, 117, 120, 127, 129-132, 136, 142-144, 146

Rhymes, 53-55, 57-61, 68, 72, 78, 83, 87, 91, 95, 99, 105, 107, 110, 113, 121, 128, 134, 138-139, 143, 145

See 2 4s, 75-78, 81, 88, 91, 96-97, 104, 107, 109, 113, 118, 121, 127, 132, 134, 136-137, 140, 143

STRETCH, 119-122, 126, 132, 135-136, 138-140, 142, 144-145

Think of 7 x 7, 125-128, 131, 133-137, 141-142, 145-146

Zero, 13-16, 18, 23, 26, 30, 34-35, 39, 42, 51, 53, 57, 63, 71, 78, 84, 87, 89, 99, 102, 122, 133, 137, 144

Multiplication Facts Listed by Name

1 Group

1×1, 1×2, 1×3, 1×4, 1×5, 1×6, 1×7, 1×8, 1×9

2×1, 3×1, 4×1, 5×1, 6×1, 7×1, 8×1, 9×1

4 Fingers

4×3, 3×4

4×4

4×5, 5×4

4×6, 6×4

4×7, 7×4

4×8, 8×4

Count by 3s

3×3

3×6, 6×3

Count 5, 6, 7, 8

7×8, 8×7

Doubles

2×2, 2×3, 2×4, 2×5

3×2, 4×2, 5×2

2×6, 2×7, 2×8, 2×9

6×2, 7×2, 8×2, 9×2

Fives

5×3, 3×5

5×4, 4×5

5×6, 6×5

5×8, 8×5

5×7, 7×5

I See 2 5s

5×5

Pretend to Add

7×7

8×8

Pretend to Add with 9

9×9

7×9, 9×7

4×9, 9×4

6×9, 9×6

5×9, 9×5

8×9, 9×8

3×9, 9×3

Rhymes

6×6

6×8, 8×6

See 2 4s

3×8, 8×3

STRETCH

3×7, 7×3

Think of 7×7

6×7, 7×6

Zero

1×0, 2×0, 3×0, 4×0, 5×0, 6×0, 7×0, 8×0, 9×0

0×1, 0×2, 0×3, 0×4, 0×5, 0×6, 0×7, 0×8, 0×9,

0×0